MW00484070

KITCHEN WIZARD

Flexipes

Volume 1

Simple Time-Saving Secrets for
Tasty Global Cuisine

Mari Suzuki
the Kitchen Wizard

Praise for Flexipes

"As an athlete, eating right is a must, but finding time to cook is always a challenge. Mari's beautiful new cookbook not only delivers easy, healthy, and delicious recipes with a Japanese twist, but walks you through the entire process of meal-planning, shopping, and preparation. Her simple "Flexipes" technique will be indispensable building blocks to a healthier lifestyle for years to come."

— **Natalie Coughlin Hall**
Three time Olympic gold medalist

"*Flexipes* may become a common culinary term as well as the hottest new cookbook to hit the shelves. Mari Suzuki's beautiful book demystifies meal planning, as you learn to fill your freezer with building blocks of healthy international flavors. This book will be a great resource for both the culinary expert or educator and the interested novice."

— **Alison Negrin**
Executive Chef, John Muir Health System
Former Chef, Chez Panisse
Founding Executive Chef, Bridges Restaurant

"Mari has created a book that is as beautiful as it is practical, reflecting her artist's soul and her systems engineer's mind. Her plan-ahead method will help you get a homemade meal on the table in record time—night after night."

— **Julie Kaufmann**
Co-author of the bestselling Not Your Mother's Slow-Cooker Cookbook *and* The Ultimate Rice Cooker Cookbook

"Mari's beautiful and thoughtful cookbook simplifies meal planning and kitchen efficiency, making it a must-have tool for every home cook."

— **Marina Kercher**
Culinary Center Director, Whole Foods Market, Napa

"In this ingenious cookbook, Mari imparts the wisdom of a true master of efficiency. If you've ever felt like you're spending too much time in the kitchen, or wondered how some people seem to create delicious dishes with almost no effort, this book is for you. A delightful read, sprinkled with beautiful photos and a lifetime of sage cooking advice."

— **Wona Miniati**
Author, Cooking With Trader Joe's Cookbook *series*

"Based on simple techniques from traditional Japanese kitchens, Mari has devised an efficient system for busy people who want fresh, flavorful meals but don't have much time for daily cooking. Using seven foundation recipes that you make ahead, she guides you through 23 delicious dishes from various culinary cultures that are versatile, healthful, and quick to prepare. Along with the dishes, Mari's tips on seasoning, stocking ingredients, and planning meals contribute to stress-free and satisfying home cooking."

— **MM Pack**
Food writer and private chef
Contributor, Austin Chronicle, Edible Austin

"This cookbook makes your mouth water and your imagination soar with fresh, easy ideas. Somebody finally gets how to make home cooking simple and healthy! Thank you, Mari—I will definitely use these simple techniques to help my students."

— **Cindy Gershen**
Chef/Owner, Sunrise Bistro
Founder, Wellness City Challenge
Contra Costa County Regional Occupational
Program Teacher for Healthy Eating in Schools

"Mari has done it! She has broken down cooking into approachable, easy steps with healthy, delicious recipes. This book can help you make the leap from a diet of fast food to eating healthy food that can be prepared fast. Never be intimidated by your kitchen again!"

— **Jen Matthews, MD**
Pediatrician and healthy food advocate

"A simple and well thought-out method to cooking in a busy world."

— **Glen Bolosan**
Owner and General Manager, Olea Restaurant

— **Gabriel Amaya**
Owner and Executive Chef, Olea Restaurant

"A must-have cookbook in the American kitchen! Mari has successfully cracked the code for those, especially working moms, who want to get back to real food but are challenged with time. *Kitchen Wizard Flexipes,* with its stunning photography and user-friendly layout, empowers its users to prepare meals that are real, fresh, home-cooked, and only minutes away!"

— **Shane Valentine**
Author, The Baby Cuisine Cookbook

KITCHEN WIZARD

Flexipes

Volume 1

Simple Time-Saving Secrets for
Tasty Global Cuisine

Mari Suzuki
the Kitchen Wizard

Kitchen Wizard Flexipes
Volume 1
Simple Time-Saving Secrets for
Tasty Global Cuisine

Copyright © 2011 Mari Suzuki
Copyright © 2011 Photographs by
Noriko Shiota and Andrew Slusser

ISBN: 978-0-9848041-0-8
ISBN: 978-0-9848041-1-5 (EPub)

Dedication

This book is dedicated to the American people who welcomed me so graciously as a resident. These recipes —or *Flexipes,* as I like to call them—are a product of my upbringing in Japanese kitchens and my cultivated love of global cuisine. *Kitchen Wizard Flexipes* is my gift to you, so that you too can cook, eat, and thrive—enjoying good food along with a healthy and long life… just like the Japanese.

To my family in Japan who taught me that home-cooked food is the highest expression of love and care. I fondly remember all the fabulous food I grew up with. I still recreate those dishes often, reliving the happy memories we shared together, which helps me feel closer to all of them, even though we now live 5,000 miles apart.

Acknowledgements

To write a book for the first time is a big endeavor. To write a full-color cookbook with a photo on almost every page is an even bigger undertaking. To do so in one's second language is an even bigger adventure still that requires a lot of people's help along the way. This book is a result of many individuals' generous help and I am forever grateful.

First and foremost, the following four people waved their magic wands to turn my idea—a rough diamond—into the gem you have in your hand.

Ayumi Kase, for designing such a beautiful layout as a foundation that helps my readers understand a new concept more clearly, and as a background for the messages and photos to shine.

Joslyn Hamilton, from Outside Eye Consulting, for ensuring my book is grammatically correct, significantly improving the reader's enjoyment, and bringing clarity and life to my words and stories.

Noriko Shiota Slusser and Andrew Slusser, for giving life to my recipes and allowing readers to taste the food with their eyes, inspiring them to awaken their inner Kitchen Wizards.

I am blessed to have these people who not only supported me in various ways but believed in me and the power of Flexipes. This book was made possible simply because of all of you. Thank you for your expertise, patience, and generosity.

To Lidia Bastianich (the best cooking show host and cookbook author, in my opinion) for allowing me to feature your delicious Swiss Chard and Potato recipe as one of my Flexipe bases in this book. To my friend, Chef Takeshi Kogure in Tokyo, for encouraging me to pursue my dream by writing a food blog, and for sharing your healthy *Nimono* recipe as another Flexipe favorite.

Countless others have helped me in many areas. For providing valuable feedback, wisdom, and editing help, I would like to thank Andrew Neuman, Lili Rollins, Doug MacLean, Tomi and Jan Sysmans, Eric Friedman, and Mylene Morgendorff. My special thanks also goes to my recipe testers—MM Pack, Karen Breeck, Keiko Takenaka, Elaine Wu, Phyllis Ginsberg, Connie Ray, Lisa Nichols, Judith Ward, Craig Ness, Rebecca Rapaport, Chris Nakashima, Nancy Satoda, Maureen Nagle, and Winona Wilson —for testing my recipes, for their enthusiasm, and for giving me reassurance that my Flexipes concept really works!

To my friend Yuko Sato of Nama-ya for loaning me your original handcrafted ceramics that allow my food to be the star.

To all of my students and blog readers who have been following me and enthusiastically kept asking me when my book was coming. This book is especially for you.

To my friends, Shane and Chantal Valentine, who convinced me to write a cookbook, and thought that for today's overwhelmed home cooks, a smaller book of my Kitchen Wizardry would be more desirable than the Harry-Potter-size publication I thought I had to write.

To my family back in Japan, for teaching me the importance of great health, and shaping my passion for both healthy and delicious food. Especially to my grandma Kimi, for trusting me as your sous chef when I was a mere 3 years old (especially in the tasting department). To my aunt Michiko, for introducing me to cuisine from around the world since I was a young girl.

Last but not least, to my husband, Keith Meyer, for your generous support, company, and encouragement. You are my marketing consultant, sales person, technical helper, English teacher, editor, coach, cultural advisor, guinea pig, taste-tester, chauffeur, sounding board, dish washer, grocery shopper, and my sous chef and a Kitchen Wizard when I'm not around. You continue to give me more than I can give back. You are the anchor to a free spirit like me when all I want is to run on the waves! Without you, this book would simply not have been possible.

Ponyo Sosuke Daisuki!

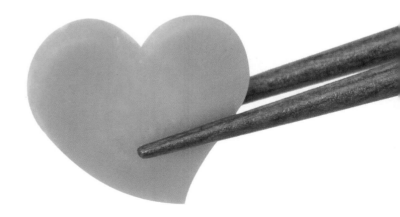

ありごま

ORGANIC

ひじ

くきわか

Contents

*My skill comes from
a simple love of good
food and a traditional
upbringing in a
Japanese home*

Mari's Story

My friends and students call me "the Kitchen Wizard." I'm confident, organized, and efficient in the kitchen, able to whip up delicious home-made meals in minutes with what I have on hand. But really, I'm just like you. I'm not a professionally trained chef, don't have a culinary degree, and have never worked in a restaurant. My skill comes from a simple love of good food and a traditional upbringing in a Japanese home, where I learned from my family how to cook healthy, delicious meals with limited time and space.

Today, I am a cookbook author and teach unique Japanese kitchen techniques to a worldwide audience through my classes and blog. But this wasn't always the case.

I used to live in kitchen chaos—disorganized, inefficient, and overwhelmed. My husband and I love good food. I was a pretty good cook, but for years, it took me forever to make dinner. As a solution for my inefficiency and lack of variety, we relied on restaurants and pre-made foods that caused us to be broke, overweight, and tired all the time. My cholesterol was high and I even became pre-diabetic, and was very close to being put on medication. This terrified me, because my own father died of diabetes at the height of his career as a doctor. So, I tried everything to eat healthier—30-minute recipes, American cooking classes, fancy new kitchen gadgets—but nothing worked… until I re-discovered the Japanese cooking secrets of my family.

Japan is known for two things: Efficiency, and lean nutritious tasty cuisine. In Japan—particularly in Tokyo, where I grew up—kitchens are much smaller than the average American kitchen. A typical Japanese kitchen has only two burners, a small sink, and no counter space. In addition, food is extremely expensive and most people don't have room for a lot of specialized kitchen appliances—not even an oven or dishwasher. But Japanese people love creative, delicious food, so it's an art form to be able to make multiple unique and enticing meals from just a few ingredients and a limited amount of space. Out of necessity, busy Japanese home cooks have developed very efficient methods that allow them to feed themselves well every day, without wasting anything.

After I adapted these tricks to my cooking here in the U.S., I was able to instantly transform myself into a "Kitchen Wizard." It became so easy and fun to "wave my magic wand" and whip up a variety of fresh, delicious meals every night with virtually no effort, no repeats, and no waste. I soon realized that these cooking secrets of my home country can be applied just as easily to any type of cuisine. With this new sense of empowerment in the kitchen, I began to use the magic of Kitchen Wizardry to restore my health, weight, and energy level. I'm happy to report that my cholesterol and blood sugar are now normal. I feel like I'm 25 again! And best of all, my husband and I saved $9,000 in the first year alone as a result of eating out less and making the most of what we already had on hand!

If I could turn my kitchen skills and my eating habits around, so can you. I hope you enjoy learning my cooking secrets so that you too can become a Kitchen Wizard.

Introduction

Frequent home-cooked meals don't always have to mean spending a lot of time in the kitchen. Discovering ways to multiply the value of what you already have in your pantry—including leftovers—can be the best cooking solution to stay efficient, economical, and eco-friendly. This book will teach you how to cook using Japan's best-kept secret: Making one dish into a variety of dishes with minimal time, effort, and cost. You'll find simple methods and recipes called Flexipes (or flex-ible rec-ipes), along with creative tricks and tips to make everyday cooking much easier and more fun.

As you now know from my story, many of my friends and family refer to me as a "Kitchen Wizard" because I am so good at waving my magic wand and creating fresh, delicious, home-cooked meals with simple ingredients I have on hand. You, too, can learn to be a Kitchen Wizard: Someone who can whip up a great meal, seemingly out of thin air, and have fun doing it. A Kitchen Wizard uses imagination and creativity to cook a great meal with limited resources, space, and time. The key to activating your own magic wand is to learn a few basic secrets and recipe bases.

The first part of this book "Quick Start Guide: Ready-To-Go Kitchen" introduces my Kitchen Wizard Methods on how to keep your kitchen and ingredients "ready to go." Having a prepared kitchen is half the battle in minimizing meal prep time and stress.

The second and core part of this book explains my original *Kitchen Wizard Flexipes*. These bases and recipes are designed to make more than one meal from a single base. It's a smarter, more convenient, and more efficient way to cook. You can pre-make Flexipe bases in large batches from scratch, and use them to whip up quick, magically delicious meals throughout the week. You'll also boost your confidence and the variety of meals you're making in your kitchen.

Sample Flexipes

Flexipe Base ▼

Day 1: Tomato & Onion Sauce (with Chicken)

» **Day 2:** Shrimp w/ Chilli Tomato Sauce

» **Day 3:** Potato Curry

» **Day 4:** Ratatouille

» **Day 5:** Fried Rice

» **Day 6:** Spicy Spanish Omelet

» **Day 7:** Chicken Vegetable Soup

30 minutes cooking time

15 minutes cooking time for each dish

With seven Flexipe bases, plus derivative recipes and other uses featured in this book, you'll be able to mix and match for endless possibilities and maximum time-saving. You can easily make meals for an entire month without ever repeating a dish.

This short cookbook will be deceptively powerful in your culinary life. It's so simple to learn, it's almost like magic! That's my Kitchen Wizard promise. You can be a Kitchen Wizard too in no time!

What exactly is the Kitchen Wizard Method?

The Kitchen Wizard Method is based on the secrets that all home cooks in Japan utilize to keep their kitchen efficient and their meals delicious and full of variety. These techniques and the Flexipes in this book are geared toward busy individuals and families who struggle in the kitchen with a lack of time, a desire for more variety, and lots of wasted food. It's a simpler, more flexible way to cook, eat, and thrive.

The Kitchen Wizard Method is an updated version of the traditional Japanese home cooking techniques I learned from my family in Tokyo. Japanese home cooks have come up with an efficient and organized way to whip up a large variety of dishes with what they already have on hand in their kitchen, without wasting a thing. This unique way of cooking allows 95% of Japanese homes to cook dinner every night of the week and waste only 3.7% of the food they buy.* In the U.S., we throw away a much higher percentage of food, on average 17%.** This is a reflection of wasted time, effort, and money in the kitchen. And the more we waste, the less we feel it's worth cooking for ourselves.

The Kitchen Wizard Method and Flexipes in particular are Japan's best-kept secret for a long, healthy life filled with great food! By redesigning the culinary wisdom of my native country for today's busy lifestyles, I hope you will feel empowered to cook more healthy and tasty food in half the time and effort every day.

This may seem like a completely new way to cook. Or, perhaps it feels more like getting back to the basics you already knew. People have been cooking this way for centuries in the East—long before the wide availability of pre-made foods and the millions of recipes in cookbooks, or on the internet.

Kitchen Wizard Flexipes is not just another cookbook full of recipes. It's a shift in the way you operate in your kitchen. Once you learn a few flexible master recipe bases, you'll be able to start playing with ingredients and discovering your own inner Kitchen Wizard.

After all, if the Japanese can do it in their tiny kitchens, so can you!

The Impact of Frequent Home-Cooked Meals (U.S. vs. Japan)

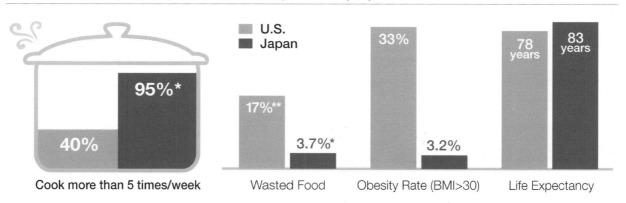

Sources: Ministry of Forestry, Fishery and Agriculture (Japanese)
TEPCO Survey 2010 (Japanese)
World Health Organization World Health Report 2004
Anon (2005)
OECD Factbook: Economic, Environmental and Social Statistics
Harris Interactive

Quick Start Guide:
Ready-To-Go Kitchen

A lot of us believe that simply having a collection of recipes is enough to get good food on the table fast. But the truth is, recipes are only half the battle. They can be great for a single meal, but most are too complicated and time-consuming for busy people to make on a daily basis. Many of us end up in a vicious cycle of dining out, eating pre-made foods, and compromising our health and well-being.

The best way to optimize our daily cooking routine is to keep everything, tools and ingredients alike, in a "ready to go" state—to maximize what we have on hand, and let the kitchen process flow as efficiently and flexibly as possible. Every time we have trouble finding an item in the kitchen—whether it's ingredients, tools, or an instruction in a recipe—we break our flow and get frustrated. By keeping our kitchen stocked with staples that are versatile and less perishable, we can minimize last-minute shopping and meal-time stress.

Storing food—keep visible, accessible, and ready to go

Refrigerator

Have several varieties of containers available in different sizes. Square or rectangular shapes are the most space efficient.

Divide your food items into ready-to-use sizes and shapes based on your needs and preferences, then wrap tightly with plastic wrap and refrigerate. For example, for a family of 2, make ½-pound packages of ground meat. When you have guests, grab more. This trick saves you overall time, ensures proper portion size, and is a must before freezing your food.

Freezer

Freezing thin items: Frozen Flexipe Flats
(Flexipe bases; other thin, batch-prepped items as seen on "The Basics of Batch Prepping" on page 22)

1. Spread about 1½ cups of food about ¼ inch thin in a quart-sized, re-sealable freezer bag so that it will be easier to break off just the amount you need when it's frozen.

2. If the food in the bag ends up a little thicker, score a grid on the bag with a chopstick or the straight edge of a rubber spatula before freezing to facilitate breaking off the right amount.

3. Freeze bags flat to keep their shape.

4. Once frozen, store them upright like books so that everything is easy to see and easy to grab.

Freezing bulkier items
(Steamed vegetables, chicken drum sticks, etc.)

1. Freeze on a cookie sheet lined with parchment paper or silicon mat, leaving some space between each item. Make sure to freeze flat, so that food won't stick.

2. When partially frozen, transfer the items to re-sealable freezer bags, and take the air out to avoid frost.

3. If you freeze different things on the same sheet pan, use one (or more) bag per item for maximum time-savings later.

Note: When freezing the individual-sized packages *(see Refrigerator section on the previous page)*, store them in freezer bags, with air taken out, to preserve freshness.

Labeling

This is one of the best time-saving tips I have to offer! Always label containers with the contents, the date prepped or reheated, and the amount (if necessary). You don't need a fancy labeling machine for this. Just use a magic marker and some masking tape. Keep them handy somewhere close to the refrigerator.

The easier and more accessible they are, the more likely you are to consistently label your containers. Once something is frozen, it's difficult to identify what it is. Frozen chicken stock looks, tastes, and smells very similar to frozen vegetable broth.

General organizing

Always think about maximum visibility and accessibility when organizing. Keep labels facing front in your refrigerator, freezer, and pantry so that you know what's there at a glance. As a rule of thumb, place perishables, small items, and things you plan to use right away toward the front for easy access. Keep longer-lasting things and larger items in the back.

For thin packages, including Frozen Flexipe Flats, store together upright like books in a rectangular container with the labels on the spine facing front for easiest access.

Use rectangular containers as make-shift drawers to organize similar things and improve accessibility. Move your shelves if necessary.

Tips for optimal kitchen flow

❶ *Grocery Shopping & Pantry Upkeep*

Always keep a master pantry and shopping list on the refrigerator door. Before things run out, or when a special event shows up on your calendar, jot down what you need. Don't rely on your memory when you get to the store; bring your list with you and buy accordingly. Sticking to a system like this means you can say goodbye to "Oops! I forgot to buy butter, again!"

For a master pantry list sample, visit
http://eepurl.com/gdS3P

❷ *Menu Planning*

Think ahead: Have a general idea of what's for dinner over the next few days based on what you have already prepped. This way you can save maximum time and money without making an elaborate meal plan every day.

For example, on Day 1, make a large batch of boiled potatoes for dinner. Cook much more than you actually need for just this meal. Day 2, turn the leftovers into mashed potatoes. Day 3, transform the leftover mashed potatoes into potato croquette. Day 4, use in shepherd's pie. And Day 5, add broth and make potato soup.

You've now shortened and streamlined your cooking process and you get to enjoy five different dishes without repeats or leftovers! This ability to turn one ingredient into multiple meals is *the* most efficient and effective secret weapon in the kitchen. It will help you decide what's for dinner so much quicker, and put food on the table that much faster.

❸ *Prepping*

Invest in good cooking tools, especially those you use every day. The most important tools in the kitchen are:

- A sharp, high-quality chef's knife
- A very large cutting board
- Several, flexible cutting mats (11" x 15" or larger)

Having sharp knives is crucial to any well-functioning kitchen. Dull knives are not only dangerous—they tend to cut your fingers instead of the food—they are hard to work with and take the fun out of cooking.

For a list of my favorite time-saving tools, check out
http://KitchenWizardMari.com/resources/tools

Cut your food thin and small so it cooks faster. Or use vegetables or cuts that require minimum washing, trimming, or cooking time.

When prepping something, always make extra—especially food that takes time to clean, such as leeks. *(The basics of batch prepping, page 22).*

Always keep some Flexipe bases as "workhorse" bases *(see next chapter)* and some basic items in your refrigerator, freezer, and pantry, so that when you don't have time to shop or prep, you can just assemble and heat up something new with what you already have.

❹ *Cooking*

Keep each type of tool close to where you will most likely use them. You'll save lots of time by not having to search any more.

A microwave or a toaster oven can shorten cooking time significantly and save energy costs. If your household is small, consider investing in a multi-function toaster oven. This will allow you to cook a whole chicken, lasagna, or medium pizza without having to pre-heat your oven.

Use your timer! It will set you free! Keep small post-it notes nearby so you can write down what you need to do when the time is up (especially when you set multiple timers at once).

❺ *Cleaning*

Wipe the grease and food residue off of your plates, pots, and pans with a paper towel first, then wash them with soap and water. This reduces the amount of water and time you use—as well as your frustration.

For cleaning tough grease, rub some detergent directly onto the greasy surface after wiping with a paper towel. Pour some hot water (use the hottest that your container can tolerate) to cover the gunk. Let it soak until the water cools off while you finish cleaning other dishes.

Improvise and experiment!

Use a recipe as a guideline or springboard. Referring back to the cookbook often breaks the flow and wastes a lot of time. We often realize that some of the ingredients are missing after we start preparing. Running to the store or changing the menu at that point (or resorting to eating out) is a waste of time and money, and leads to stress. Instead, experiment! If you like the taste of something, add a little more. Don't be afraid! The results could be different, but who knows—you might like it better than the original. Just jot down the results of your experiment directly in this book, so that you know what to do next time.

What can you do now to save time later?

We all unconsciously waste time in the kitchen because we don't take the time to make it more organized and efficient. For busy people, the best way to set yourself up for a well-flowing kitchen is to take the time now to create a good system. Then, when you are in a hurry to cook, everything will be ready for you. Invest the time and energy setting up a Ready-To-Go Kitchen now. It will pay dividends immediately. If you can save yourself even fifteen minutes a day, at the end of a year you will have saved over ninety hours of time. That's over eleven work days at the office!

And here's the good news: Setting up a Ready-To-Go Kitchen is simple. It doesn't take much, and can be done one step at a time. You can start by choosing a tip or two that interest you, see how easy it is, and go from there.

The basics of batch prepping

Let's quickly walk through a few batch prepping basics that will help you start saving time right away.

As a guideline, raw items should keep fresh in the refrigerator for a few days. Cooked items last up to 1 week. Frozen items will keep about 1 month. It all depends on conditions like temperature, handling, and freshness of the original ingredients. So always use your common sense—if it looks, smells, or taste strange, TOSS.

Chopped Onions, Leeks, and Green Onions (Raw, Sauteed, or Caramelized)

Chopped onions, both raw and cooked, are basic ingredients in so many recipes, including salads, dressings, sandwiches, salsas, chili toppings, and burger toppings. You can also sauté and use onions in many sauces, soups, braised dishes, fried rice, stuffing, pizza, meatballs, and more.

When you have time, do tedious tasks—like cleaning leeks or caramelizing onions—all at once. Use some, and keep the rest as Frozen Flexipe Flats *(page 18)*. Just break off as much as you need and throw in as a flavor booster.

Chopped green onions are especially handy for Asian dishes. Just chop them up and store in the refrigerator or freezer for later.

The most flexible forms are:

- **Onions:** Sliced thin (¼ inch slivers) or chopped (¼ inch). Raw, sautéed, or caramelized.
- **Leeks:** Dark green part trimmed, quartered lengthwise with the bottom intact, cleaned, and sliced to ¼ inch thickness. Sautéed.
- **Green onions:** Sliced thin (1/4 inch). Raw.

Cut Vegetables (Raw, Sautéed, Steamed or Blanched)

When you're prepping vegetables, wash and cut more than you need, and refrigerate or freeze the rest. This way, they are ready to go as a healthy snack, lunch accompaniment, or salad standby. When we have these healthy alternatives on hand, we tend to eat them instead of high calorie snacks and convenience foods, helping us build healthier eating habits.

If your recipe calls for blanching or sautéing, consider cooking extra. Undercook slightly for best color, flavor, and later versatility. They are handy bases for side dishes and soups.

Vegetables should be prepped and cut in their most flexible form:

- **Celery, zucchini, cucumbers, peppers:** Thin sticks, ½ inch by 3 inches. Raw.
- **Carrots:** Thin sticks, ½ inch by 3 inches. Raw, sautéed, steamed, or blanched.
- **Broccoli, cauliflower:** Bite-sized florets. Raw, sautéed, steamed, or blanched.
- **Asparagus, green beans:** Trimmed and cut to 3 inches. Raw, sautéed, steamed, or blanched.

Store each type of vegetable in a separate container for easy picking and choosing later.

Cooked, Shredded Chicken

You can use fresh or frozen chicken.

1. Sprinkle salt and white wine or *sake* on both sides of the chicken and let marinate while boiling water. Chicken tenderloins can be left as is. It's a busy person's best friend! If using breast or thigh meat, cut the thickness in half or into bite-sized pieces first, so that they cook faster and more evenly.

2. Add chicken to plenty of boiling salted water, with a few extra tablespoons of wine or *sake* until the chicken is cooked through. (If using frozen chicken, make sure that you have a lot of boiling water, and cover with a lid to bring it back to a boil again, so that the temperature of the water doesn't go down too much.)

3. Once the chicken is cooked through without a trace of pink inside, pull it out and shred with two forks. Save the remaining liquid as a base for soups.

Tip: Chicken prepared this way can be used for pastas, noodles, salads, sandwiches, or soups… in other words, for practically any type of cuisine. Alternatively, you can shred the leftover cooked or rotisserie chicken to save even more time. Make sure you choose a lightly seasoned variety so that it won't affect the flavor of the dishes you will be making later.

Steamed Rice

Works well with white, brown, or mixed rice.

1. Make a large batch of rice, use some, and wrap the rest in plastic while still warm into ½ to ¾ cup-size individual packages. When they reach room temperature, store in a freezer bag.

2. When you need cooked rice, pour water over the package to remove plastic wrap, place frozen rice in a deep bowl, cover, and microwave on high for a few minutes until hot. It's convenient, and tastes just as good as freshly steamed rice.

Flexipes: Bases and Recipes

Building blocks: 1 base, many dishes… save time and money

To introduce you to the concept of Kitchen Wizard Flexipes, each section features a different Flexipe base and 3 to 5 dishes you can prepare from each base. Some of them re-appear in later sections to show their flexibility.

I encourage you to learn to cook with what you have on hand—without relying on thousands of recipes, or making everyday cooking more complicated than necessary. Use the recipes in this book not as a rule set in stone, but as a guideline in terms of amounts and ingredients. By trusting your five senses—sight, smell, sound, touch, and most importantly taste—you will become a confident, competent cook much faster. You'll be surprised how well your food turns out and how much faster you can put the meal on the table when you cook intuitively. Plus it's fun and relaxing to cook this way. It's like child's play! You add extra S&P to the all dishes you make… Smile and Play, that is. They are the best spices of all!

About Flexipe portions: You may find the portions of my recipes lighter than what you are used to. I also use more vegetables compared to meat or carbohydrates. This ratio is how we traditionally eat in Japan, and is similar to the new recommended daily allowances for optimal health in the U.S.

I recommend serving a bowl of salad or side dish made with various pre-prepped vegetables *(page 22)* to round out the meal. Finish your meal with some fruit. The great thing is, you can eat as many vegetables and fruits as you like!

Tips for successfully using Flexipes

Each Flexipe base in this book is enough to make 2 to 3 recipes for 2 people. Make the base first, eat some, then use the remainder to make other recipes to experience the efficiency and convenience. To serve more, double or triple the recipe by using a larger pan or multiple pots. Just remember to taste frequently and adjust seasoning as you go.

The sub-headers in each recipe outlining the main steps will help you follow the recipe and learn the basic flow.

To maximize time and minimize waste, be sure to utilize the batch prepping basics you learned in the previous chapter *(page 22)*, especially when "pre-prepped vegetables" or "vegetables you have on hand" are called for in the recipes.

General cutting and cooking tips: Cut each ingredient into a uniform size to ensure even cooking. The smaller or thinner you chop your longer-cooking vegetables, the shorter the cooking time. When cooking vegetables, start from those that take the longest to cook (normally the hardest ones like root vegetables), then continue in that order. Add the tender, quick-cooking vegetables such as corn, leafy greens, and bean sprouts last, or right before you turn off the heat.

Shelf life of Flexipe bases: Most vegetable Flexipe bases should keep up to 1 week in the refrigerator, and up to 1 month in the freezer. (For freezing instructions, see *page 18*.)

For meat bases, see *pages 62 and 68*.

Note: Freezing the Potato and Swiss Chard Base *(page 40)* is not recommended—the potatoes will get spongy. If you want to keep this or any other base in the refrigerator longer, reheat completely or make into another cooked dish.

By trusting your five senses—sight, smell, sound, touch, and most importantly taste—you will become a confident, competent cook much faster.

FLEXIPE BASE 1.

Tomato and Onion Base

- Turkish Green Beans with Light Tomato Sauce
- Shrimp with Chili Sauce
- Indian Curry

Many people associate tomato sauce with Italian cuisine. However, many other cultures also use something similar in their cooking. An Italian version we are familiar with is made with lots of tomatoes and garlic, and a little bit of onion, if any. My tomato and onion sauce is quite different. It's well-flavored with lots of onions, so it's not only for pastas and chicken, but a perfect base for ethnic favorites such as ratatouille, curries, shrimp with chili sauce, risottos, and more. I even use it as a condiment, a sandwich spread, or even as pizza sauce.

As you can see, many tomato dishes call for sautéed onions anyway, so you will find this version both versatile and convenient. You can use yellow, white, or even red onions in the base.

If possible, use fresh, ripe tomatoes for this base; it will give a better balance of tomato and onion, and taste much fresher and more flavorful. For maximum nutrition and time-savings, the skins and seeds can be chopped and added to the sauce.

Makes about 3 cups

- ▶ 2 to 3 tablespoons vegetable oil
- ▶ 4 cloves garlic, minced
- ▶ 2 medium onions, diced ¼ to ½ inch
- ▶ About 2 pounds fresh ripe tomatoes (or 1 large can = 28 ounces), chopped
- ▶ Salt and pepper to taste

❶ *Cook Onion* » Heat oil in a large skillet over medium heat. Cook minced garlic until fragrant. Add chopped onions and a little salt. Cook until soft and lightly browned over medium-high heat, stirring occasionally, about 5 minutes.

❷ *Cook Tomatoes* » Add chopped tomatoes and cook until most of the moisture evaporates and the mixture takes on a thick saucy texture, about 5 to 10 minutes. Taste and adjust seasoning with salt and pepper.

Turkish Green Beans with Light Tomato Sauce

Turkish green beans are a part of typical *mezze* (a traditional appetizer spread) in Turkey and Greece. When my husband and I visited Turkey, we ate it all the time and never got bored with it. This dish is usually served cold, but is delicious hot as well. Ideal for parties, you can make it ahead of time and not worry about re-heating it.

This is also a great twist on ordinary Thanksgiving green beans. Try it—everyone will love it! When cooking for a potluck, make enough so that you can save some for yourself. Turkish green beans taste great for days.

Tip: A squeeze of lemon juice or some extra virgin olive oil at the end enhances the flavor, especially when eaten cold.

Serves 2 to 3

- ▶ 2 to 3 tablespoons extra virgin olive oil
- ▶ About 1 pound green beans, ends removed, cut or broken into 2 to 3 inch pieces
- ▶ About ⅓ to ½ cup **TOMATO & ONION BASE** *(p.28)*
- ▶ ½ teaspoon sugar
- ▶ Salt and pepper to taste
- ▶ 4 to 5 fresh basil leaves or a pinch of dry basil
- ▶ Optional: ½ teaspoon tomato purée
- ▶ About 1 cup boiling water

❶ *Sauté Green Beans* » Heat oil in a medium sauce pan. Add green beans, **Tomato & Onion Base**, sugar, salt, and pepper. Stir and cook on medium-high heat until the green beans begin to soften.

❷ *Braise* » Add tomato puree, basil, and boiling water to barely cover the beans. Stirring occasionally, cook uncovered until vegetables are soft and most of the water is evaporated, about 15 to 20 minutes. Taste and adjust seasoning. Serve hot or cold.

Indian Curry

This Flexipe is built upon the Tomato and Onion Base, and it's also a base on its own. It's versatile and can be used in many different dishes to add a delicious curry flavor.

My version has the flavor of Indian curry without the labor-intensive cooking time and the hard-to-find ingredients.

Just split up the Indian curry base, and add different types of vegetables or proteins to whip up as many variations as you like! The choices are endless, limited only by your imagination and what you have on hand.

Examples:

- **Vegetables:** Potato, cauliflower, eggplant, spinach, pumpkin
- **Vegetarian protein:** Beans (lentils, chickpeas), *paneer* cheese, boiled eggs
- **Meat:** Chicken, beef, lamb, ground meat with green peas
- **Seafood:** Fish, shrimp, mixed seafoods

Makes about 1½ cups of curry base:
enough for 2 kinds of curry for 2 people, or 1 kind for 4

- ▶ 1 to 2 tablespoons vegetable oil (increase the amount if you are using more spices)
- ▶ ½ inch fresh ginger, peeled, minced (about 1 tablespoon)
- ▶ 1 tablespoon or more curry powder
- ▶ ½ teaspoon or more cumin powder
- ▶ Optional: ½ teaspoon or more cayenne powder
- ▶ 1 teaspoon or more **garam masala** (available in the spice section)
- ▶ 1½ cups **TOMATO & ONION BASE** *(p.28)*
- ▶ 1½ cups total of your favorite cooked vegetables, meat and/or seafood (per 2 servings)
- ▶ About ½ to 1 cup water (per 2 servings)
- ▶ Salt and pepper
- ▶ 2 cups steamed rice, or 2 pieces **naan** bread

❶ *Cook Spices* ❯❯ Heat oil in a medium skillet on medium heat. Add minced ginger, cook briefly, then add the spices. The amount of spices listed makes a mildly spicy curry. If you like it spicier, increase the amount of ginger and spices, and/or add cayenne. Stir well until the mixture becomes fragrant and forms a smooth paste.

❷ *Make Curry Base and Split* ❯❯ Add **Tomato & Onion Base** and cook until most of the moisture evaporates and the mixture gets a bit pasty. Taste and adjust seasoning with salt and pepper. To make 2 different curries, split this into two skillets.

❸ *Add Vegetables or Protein* ❯❯ Add a total of 1½ cups cooked vegetables or protein (see examples in the left column) to each skillet with curry. (3 cups if you did not split). Cook over medium-high heat, and adjust the thickness by gradually adding about ½ to 1 cup water. (Vegetables and meats you choose will add varying amounts of moisture to the dish, so adjust accordingly.) Taste and adjust seasoning.

❹ *Serve Hot* ❯❯ Top with chopped cilantro, if desired. Serve hot with steamed rice, *naan* bread (available in specialty stores), and/or *raita* (yogurt sauce—*page 43*).

Shrimp with Chili Sauce

This dish originated in Sichuan Province in China, and is one of the most beloved home-cooked dinners in Japan. The father of Iron Chef Chinese, Chen Kenichi (from the original, Japanese version of the show) made this dish popular. He told his TV viewers, "I may be lying, but it is a tasty lie." His dishes may not be authentic; they use more accessible ingredients and techniques, and appeal to the Japanese palette.

By using the already-prepared Tomato and Onion Base, the time to prepare this classic is shortened from 40 minutes to 15 minutes, max! It is faster, tastier, and cheaper than ordering takeout. You can substitute other kinds of seafood like scallops *(as shown in the photo above)*, or frozen seafood, chicken, or all vegetables.

Serves 2 (or 3 if you add more vegetables)

- ▶ ½ pound medium shrimp, de-veined
- ▶ ½ tablespoon *sake* or dry white wine
- ▶ ½ tablespoon corn or potato starch
- ▶ 1 tablespoon vegetable oil
- ▶ ½ inch fresh ginger, minced or grated (½ to 1 tablespoon)
- ▶ ⅓ to ½ cup **TOMATO & ONION BASE** *(p.28)*
- ▶ Optional: ½ to 1 cup pre-prepped vegetables sliced into ¼ inch or diced into ½ inch (Examples: sliced **shiitake**, bell pepper, asparagus, cooked bamboo shoot, etc.)
- ▶ 1 to 2 teaspoons chili bean paste
- ▶ 1 to 2 teaspoons oyster sauce
- ▶ Salt
- ▶ 1½ to 2 cups steamed rice

❶ *Prepare Shrimp* » Sprinkle salt and *sake* on shrimp, and lightly massage in. Pat dry and sprinkle with potato or corn starch, and toss.

❷ *Cook Spices and Vegetables* » Heat ½ tablespoon vegetable oil in a medium non-stick skillet on medium-high heat, cook ginger and chili bean paste until fragrant, stirring occasionally, about 30 seconds. Add prepped vegetables and sauté for about a minute. Season lightly with salt.

❸ *Cook Shrimp* » Push the vegetables toward the outer edge of the skillet, add another ½ tablespoon oil, and cook shrimp for a few minutes.

❹ *Season with Tomato & Onion Base* » Add **Tomato & Onion Base** and oyster sauce. Cook until sauce is thickened and shrimp turns an appetizing pink color. If you didn't add any vegetables, and/or the sauce seems too thick, add about 1 to 2 tablespoons water. Taste and adjust seasonings. Serve hot with steamed rice.

Mushroom Base

- Mushroom Spread
- Mushroom Bisque
- Chicken Marsala

I always have this base in my refrigerator or freezer, both a regular mushroom version and an Asian mushroom version (*shiitake,* king oyster, oyster, *enoki,* etc.). This sautéed sliced mushroom base is far more versatile than the traditional *duxelle* (sautéed, finely chopped mushrooms with wine). If a recipe calls for chopped mushrooms or *duxelle,* you can always chop the mushrooms smaller… but not the other way around.

Mushroom Base is a great addition to burgers, steaks, chicken, veal, pasta, risotto, polenta, quiche, crêpes, and stuffing, as well as the primary foundation of mushroom pilaf, warm mushroom salad, and mushroom soup. You can even blend it in a food processor for a tasty mushroom spread.

Many stores offer pre-sliced mushrooms and specials on not-so-perfect mushrooms that work just fine for this base. Take advantage of them. An egg slicer can be used to slice mushrooms in a snap.

Tip: For a warm mushroom salad, have some spring greens ready in a salad bowl. Top with the mushroom base straight out of the pan to wilt the greens, and dress with a little bit of balsamic vinegar, good salt, and pepper. Simply delicious and elegant!

Makes about 1½ to 2 cups

▶ 1 pound mushrooms, a single kind or mixed, sliced
▶ 1 small onion OR 1 to 2 shallots OR 2 cloves garlic
▶ Optional: 1 tablespoon herbs (thyme etc), chopped
▶ 2 tablespoons extra virgin olive oil
▶ 1 to 2 tablespoons white wine or *sake*
▶ Salt and pepper

❶ *Cook Aromatics* » Heat oil in a large skillet over medium heat. Add chopped onion, shallots, or minced garlic, cook until soft.

❷ *Cook Mushrooms* » Increase heat to medium-high. Add sliced mushrooms and a little salt to draw out their moisture. This will cut the amount of oil needed and help them cook faster. Add chopped herbs if using.

❸ *Reduce and Season* » Add white wine or *sake*. Reduce the liquid by half. Taste and adjust seasoning with salt and pepper. Serve hot.

Mushroom Spread

Once you have a mushroom base, a mushroom spread is an easy next step: Simply add about 1 cup of **MUSHROOM BASE** *(p.34)* to your food processor or blender with 1 tablespoon of extra virgin olive oil and purée until it's chunky. Taste and adjust seasoning with more oil, salt, and pepper. I like to split the spread in half, serve one as it is, and mix another one with cream cheese or goat cheese. Two appetizers for the effort of one! Start with a 2 to 1 ratio—about ½ cup pureed mushroom to ¼ cup cheese—taste and adjust the amount to your preference.

Tip: It's easier to mix if the cheese is left at room temperature for a little while.

Mushroom Bisque

This soup is so fast and flavorful, it's like magic! I often call it Magic Mushroom Soup, because all you need is sautéed Mushroom Base and milk. If your base doesn't include onion or aromatics, sauté ½ cup of chopped onion or 1 shallot first, before adding mushrooms. This bisque is also delicious with sautéed leeks or caramelized onion.

Tip: I highly recommend using an immersion blender directly in the pot when pureeing the soup for maximum safety, convenience, and time-savings. While you can use a regular blender or food processor, you'll need to wait until the soup is cool enough, *and* transfer it carefully—*twice*. This can get messy and dangerous if you're not careful!

Serves 2 to 3

▶ 1 cup **MUSHROOM BASE** *(p.34)*

▶ Optional: ¼ cup sautéed leeks or caramelized onion

▶ 1½ to 2 cups milk (OR half milk and half broth)

▶ Salt and pepper

❶ *Add Liquid to Mushrooms* » In a 1 to 2 quart sauce pan, combine milk, **Mushroom Base** and leek or caramelized onion, if using. Add broth or ½ cube of bouillon, if richer flavor is desired.

❷ *Heat and Puree* » Heat the soup over medium-high heat (do not let it boil). Puree with an immersion blender. If the soup is too thick, add more liquid and heat through. Taste and adjust seasoning. Serve hot.

Options: Top with cream or butter for richer flavor, or garnish with herbs, croutons, etc.

For a twist, add leftover potatoes (baked, boiled, or mashed) and/ or Dijon mustard and puree the soup. If your sautéed mushroom base is frozen, simply break some off, add to the pot directly, add liquid, and heat.

Chicken Marsala

In 15 minutes you can have a complete homemade meal of Chicken Marsala, *Mirepoix Pilaf (page 54)*, and salad. All you need is a few Flexipe bases from your refrigerator or freezer.

For the chicken, you can use leftover roast chicken, frozen chicken tenderloins, fresh chicken, or—for the best flavor—Flexipe Base 6, Marinated Chicken with Garlic *(page 62)*. When using fresh chicken breasts or thighs, slice them thinly so that they cook fast and evenly.

Tip: Marsala is fortified wine from the city of Marsala in Sicily. If you do not have Marsala wine, simply use wine (either red or white) or chicken stock to make Chicken with Mushroom Sauce. Or, use white wine and sour cream instead, to create Chicken Stroganoff. If you use beef instead of chicken, you guessed it, it's Beef Stroganoff.

Serves 2

- ▶ ½ pound chicken tenderloins
- ▶ 1 to 2 tablespoons white wine
- ▶ ½ to 1 tablespoon extra virgin olive oil
- ▶ ½ cup **MUSHROOM BASE** *(p.34)*
- ▶ 1 tablespoon flour
- ▶ ½ cup Marsala wine (or half Marsala and half chicken broth)
- ▶ Salt and pepper
- ▶ Optional: ½ tablespoon butter

❶ *Prepare and Cook Chicken* » Sprinkle white wine, salt, and pepper on both sides of chicken. Pat dry. Heat extra virgin olive oil in a medium skillet over medium-high heat until hot, and pan-fry chicken. When the bottom is golden brown, flip over and brown the other side. Sprinkle flour onto the pan, and stir and cook briefly.

❷ *Add Mushrooms and Wine* » Add sautéed **Mushroom Base** and wine/broth and cook down for a few minutes until the sauce is thickened. Taste and adjust seasoning. Add about ½ tablespoon butter if richer flavor is desired. Serve hot over *Mirepoix Pilaf (p.54),* egg noodles, mashed potatoes, etc.

Note: After browning the chicken, most recipes call for setting it aside to prevent overcooking while sautéing mushrooms. With this Flexipe, you can skip this step and make the *roux* and sauce all at once, while at the same time cooking the chicken.

Potato and Swiss Chard Base

- Soups
- *Tortilla Española* (Spanish Omelet)
- Potato and Swiss Chard Curry

Potato and Swiss Chard Base

Although I love using Potato and Swiss Chard as a base, it's a great stand-alone dish that can be eaten as-is. I originally found this side dish recipe in Lidia Bastianich's classic, *Lidia's Italian Table* (Publisher: William Morrow and Company). I love Lidia's recipes and stories, and I have made quite a few of them from both her book and her TV show. One day it dawned on me that I could use this as a Flexipe base! My experiments have proven to me that you can enjoy Sautéed Potato and Swiss Chard as a side dish one day and then revise it for breakfast, lunch, snacks, and dinner on following days. No one will notice that it started with the same base dish.

Examples of ways I use Potato and Swiss Chard Base: Spanish omelets, potato and Swiss chard curry (then the leftovers from this can be made into *samosas*), soups, quesadillas, crepes, potato pancakes, grilled pita sandwich... I make these things all the time, and never get tired of the basic potatoes and greens. As Lidia states in her book, the flavor of this dish improves when it's made in advance and reheated. Perfect for Kitchen Wizardry!

Thank you, Lidia, for allowing me to use your recipe as one of my Flexipe bases, to create more variety and make everyday cooking faster, easier, and tastier—until the very last bite!

Serves 6 to 8, or enough to make all these variations for 2
(Adapted from *Lidia's Italian Table* by Lidia Bastianich, Publisher: William Morrow and Company)

▶ **3 quarts water**

▶ **4 medium-sized Idaho potatoes (about 2 pounds), peeled and cut lengthwise into quarters**

▶ **1 bunch Swiss chard (about 1½ pounds), stems removed from leaves, cut both into 1 inch-wide strips**

▶ **2 to 4 tablespoons extra virgin olive oil**

▶ **3 to 4 garlic cloves, crushed**

▶ **Salt and pepper**

❶ *Boil Potatoes* » First, bring 3 quarts of water to a boil in a large (6 to 8 quart) covered pot over high heat. Clean, peel, and chop vegetables while waiting. Dissolve 2 to 3 teaspoons of salt into boiling water. Add quartered potatoes and cook uncovered for 10 minutes.

❷ *Boil Chard* » Add the chopped Swiss chard stems, then leaves, cook until tender, about 10 more minutes. Scoop the vegetables out (or drain in a colander). Save the potato water to make soup with later on *(page 41)*.

❸ *Sauté Vegetables* » In a large skillet, heat 2 tablespoons of olive oil over medium heat and cook garlic until it begins to brown. Add the drained vegetables and season lightly with salt and pepper. Cook, stirring and mashing the potatoes, until the liquid has evaporated and potatoes are coarsely mashed and lightly brown. Add remaining 2 tablespoons olive oil if desired. Taste and adjust seasoning. Serve hot.

Soups

The drained potato broth you saved from Step 2 from the previous page will create simple yet satisfying soups in minutes. Allow about 1 cup broth per person.

Potato and Chard Soup

Potato Broth Soup »
Simply add salt and pepper (to taste) to the drained potato broth and top with a little extra virgin olive oil, butter, heavy cream, or grated cheeses (Parmigiano-Reggiano, Romano, or any type that melts) to boost flavor.

Caldo Verde:
Portugal's National Soup »
Add a handful-per-person of thinly shredded cabbage or kale to the hot drained potato broth, along with slices of chorizo. Heat until the greens are tender.

Potato and Chard Soup »
Add potato broth to the **Potato & Swiss Chard Base** to cover and heat through (about ½ cup each of potato and broth per person). Double the amount and make the following:

Pureed Potato and Chard Soup »
Enjoy another variation later by using the leftover Potato and Chard Soup. Pureeing with an immersion blender minimizes time and mess. (*Optional:* add other boiled/sautéed vegetables, cream, and/or mustard for variation.) Add more broth to adjust thickness.

Pureed Potato and Chard Soup

Tortilla Española (Spanish Omelet)

This dish used to be a once a year treat, but now that I use the leftover Potato and Swiss Chard Base, *Tortilla Española* appears on our table a lot more often, especially as a breakfast or snack.

The beauty of this recipe is that because the potato and chard filling is already made and cool enough to handle, you can add the eggs right away, making it ready to eat in less than ten minutes. Plus, it uses a lot less oil. Swiss chard adds far more vitamins, minerals, calcium, and fiber than the more traditional potato and onion version.

You can also use the leftover Potato and Swiss Chard Curry *(page 43)* to make a curried version. Both are very delicious!

Serves 2 to 3

- ▸ 1½ cups **POTATO & SWISS CHARD BASE** *(p.40)*
- ▸ 3 eggs, beaten
- ▸ 1 teaspoon extra virgin olive oil
- ▸ Salt and pepper

❶ *Combine Eggs and Potatoes; Cook* » Beat eggs in a bowl. Add **Potato & Swiss Chard Base**, and season generously with salt and pepper. Heat extra virgin olive oil in an 8-inch non-stick skillet (far easier to flip than a 10-inch pan) on medium heat. Add the egg mixture and cook until egg is set and golden brown, about 3 to 4 minutes. Shake the pan or use the spatula to loosen if it sticks while cooking.

❷ *Flip Over and Cook the Other Side* » Cover with a flat, tight-fitting lid (or a plate), flip quickly (be careful—it's very hot!), and slide it back into the skillet to cook the other side. Cook about another 3 to 4 minutes, until golden brown on both sides—but

still a little soft inside. Invert the omelet onto a plate. Let stand for 5 minutes before cutting into wedges. Serve hot, at room temperature, or cold; as-is, or with mayonnaise, aioli, or *romesco* sauce (a classic Spanish pureed sauce made of garlic, almonds, grilled tomatoes and red pepper, and olive oil).

Tip: If you are nervous about flipping the omelet, or only have a 10-inch or cast iron skillet, enjoy as a frittata. *To make frittata:* Preheat oven to 450 F. Cook egg mixture in the oven-proof non-stick or cast iron skillet as in Step 1. Then transfer the skillet to the oven, bake uncovered until the eggs are firm, 7 to 10 minutes. If using a 10-inch pan, double the recipe.

Potato and Swiss Chard Curry

To make this quick, delicious curry dish, simply add the Indian Curry Base *(page 30)* to the Potato and Swiss Chard Base. This may not be the most authentic recipe (is there any Swiss chard in India?), but you will love it! Just as with *Tortilla Española (page 42)*, chard adds more nutrients to your diet than potatoes alone. It's one of the most nutritious vegetables you can eat.

If you double the recipe, you can save half to make a curried version of the *Tortilla Española (page 42)*.

Serves 2 to 3

▶ ⅔ cup Indian Curry *(on page 30)*
▶ 1½ to 2 cups **POTATO & SWISS CHARD BASE** *(p.40)*
▶ About ½ to 1 cup water or stock
▶ Optional: Chopped cilantro
▶ 1½ to 2 cups steamed rice and/or 2 *naan* bread

❶ *Cook Vegetables in Curry* » Heat the curry base in the pan over medium heat. Add **Potato & Swiss Chard Base** and some stock or water as needed (it depends on how much moisture the vegetables have, as well as your personal preference). Cook until the flavor is incorporated and heated through. Adjust seasoning.

❷ *Serve Curry* » Top with chopped cilantro, if desired. Serve with steamed rice, saffron rice, *naan* bread (available in specialty stores), and/or *raita* (yogurt sauce—*see below*).

Note: Raita is a typical accompaniment for curry in India. Simply combine diced onions (milder red onions are the best for this), cucumber, and/or tomatoes with ½ to 1 cup yogurt. Season with salt and pepper to taste. Top with chopped cilantro, a dash of paprika and/or cayenne for extra color and zest.

FLEXIPE BASE 4.

Nimono Base:
Lightly-Braised Japanese Vegetables

- *Suiton* (Chunky *Miso* Soup with Dumplings)
- *Iri-Dofu* (Tofu Scramble)
- *Takikomi-Gohan* (Japanese Mixed Rice with Root Vegetables)

Nimono Base: Lightly-Braised Japanese Vegetables

This updated version of a Japanese classic, *nimono* (braised dish) is another great base that can be eaten on its own or used as a starting point for other dishes. I learned this from my friend, the renowned Chef Kogure from Tokyo. A brief cooking time and much less sodium and sugar make this recipe ideal for today's busy, healthier lifestyles. Best of all, you can really taste the flavor of each vegetable.

Plant-based dishes like this one are one of the reasons Japanese food is considered one of the most nutritious. This dish is an easy way to boost your daily vegetable intake.

Feel free to substitute bite-sized pieces of firm vegetables like asparagus, broccoli, cauliflower, and/or quartered Brussels sprouts for any other vegetables you don't have.

Enjoy as is, or use the leftover to make gratins, curries *(page 30)*, or soups. Or chop them up to make filling or sauce for meat, fish, *tofu*, crêpes, salads, or even for pot-stickers *(page 72)*. Depending on the seasonings, you can turn this into a Western or Asian dish—you'll love it!

Makes about 7 to 8 cups, enough to eat as is, and all variations for 2 to 3

- ▸ 2 cups *daikon* radish (about 3 inches) or small white radishes, peeled
- ▸ 2 cups carrot (about 3), peeled
- ▸ 2 cups lotus root (about 1), peeled
- ▸ 2 cups green beans or snow peas, trimmed
- ▸ 1 cup fresh *shiitake* mushrooms (about 5 or 6), stems removed
- ▸ 2 tablespoons extra virgin olive oil
- ▸ 1½ tablespoons soy sauce
- ▸ 1½ tablespoons *mirin* (Japanese sweet rice wine)
- ▸ 1½ tablespoons *sake*
- ▸ Salt and pepper
- ▸ Optional: Sesame seeds

❶ *Prepare Vegetables* » Peel vegetables and cut them into uniform, bite-sized pieces. If using snow peas, just trim the ends and remove strings.

❷ *Steam Vegetables* » Add about ½ cup of water in a large skillet or sauté pan with a pinch of salt and bring to a boil over high heat. Add all vegetables (except snow peas) and cover tightly. Cook for about 5 minutes until the vegetables are glistening and crisp-tender. Take out the vegetables and place in a bowl.

❸ *Sauté Vegetables and Season* » Wipe the skillet dry, heat extra virgin olive oil over medium-high heat. Add all the vegetables (and snow peas if using), soy sauce, *mirin*, and *sake*. Sauté for a few minutes to season vegetables. Taste and adjust seasoning with salt and pepper. Serve hot or at room temperature, with sesame seeds on top as a garnish.

Suiton (Chunky *Miso* Soup with Dumplings)

This hearty, chunky soup with a lot of vegetables has regained its popularity in Japan because it's very healthy. There are many variations—the soy sauce version with tofu is called *Kenchin Jiru,* and the *miso* broth version with chicken (with bones) is called *Satsuma Jiru.* When there is more broth and less vegetables, it's simply *miso* soup!

Suiton means "dumplings in water" in Japanese, because of the flour dumplings cooked in the broth. They are strictly optional, yet very satisfying—especially when it's cold outside! The flour in these dumplings tends to thicken the soup, so make only the amount of flour mixture you would eat in one meal.

Serves 2 to 3

▶ 1 to 1½ cups NIMONO BASE *(p.46)*

▶ Optional: ½ cup total of tofu, *shiitake,* cooked pumpkin, and/or cooked chicken, cut in bite-sized pieces or smaller

▶ 3 cups Japanese *dashi* broth *(p.74),* or 3 cups water and a 3-inch square of *kombu* (sea kelp—*p.74*), or chicken broth

▶ ⅔ cup flour

▶ 1 teaspoon sesame oil

▶ ⅓ cup water

▶ 1 to 2 tablespoons *miso* (or 1 tablespoon soy sauce)

▶ 2 green onions, chopped

▶ Salt

▶ Optional: Sesame seeds or *shichimi togarashi* powder (Japanese seven spice chili powder)

❶ *Make Soup* » Add *dashi* or broth to the Nimono Base (and tofu etc. if using) in a medium saucepan and bring to a boil. (If using *kombu,* take it out when the water starts to boil.)

❷ *Add Flour Mixture in Soup* » Mix flour with water, sesame oil, and a pinch of salt in a small bowl until it's well blended and looks like soft ice cream. Drop it by the teaspoonful into the boiling soup. Adjust the heat to maintain a lively simmer.

❸ *Season* » When the dumplings float to the surface, turn down the heat to simmer and add *miso* (or soy sauce). Taste, and adjust the seasoning with more *miso* and salt, if needed. Add green onions, heat it through (do not let the soup boil after you add *miso*). Serve hot with sesame seeds or *shichimi togarashi* powder on top, if you have any.

Iri-Dofu (Tofu Scramble)

Tofu scrambles are something Japanese have been enjoying for many decades. You can experiment with different seasonings, vegetables and protein you have on hand. The most traditional version is very nutritious yet time-consuming, since it calls for many finely chopped vegetables. By using the chopped up *Nimono* Base, it's not only healthy but much faster to prepare. If you have any Italian style, high-quality tuna in olive oil, add some. It will make it even more flavorful.

Note: Microwaving tofu before cooking helps drain the moisture out of the tofu quickly. If you don't own a microwave, simply break up tofu with your hand, and stir fry over high heat with about ½ teaspoon salt without oil, until all the moisture is evaporated. In step 2, increase the amount of oil to 2 teaspoons and proceed. The extra salt and oil is to compensate for the higher water left inside; otherwise, the tofu will taste a little bland.

Serves 2 to 3

- ▶ 1 package semi-firm to firm tofu (about 14 ounces)
- ▶ Optional: ½ can tuna in olive oil (about ¼ cup), crumbled
- ▶ ½ tablespoon extra virgin olive oil (if using tuna in olive oil, use the oil from the can)
- ▶ About ½ to ¾ cup **NIMONO BASE** *(p.46)*, chopped small
- ▶ 1 tablespoon *sake*
- ▶ 1 tablespoon soy sauce
- ▶ 2 stalks green onions, chopped small
- ▶ 2 eggs, beaten

❶ *Cook Tofu* » Wrap tofu with a paper towel, and microwave 4 to 5 minutes on high. Heat a shallow pan with a wide bottom on high heat, stir fry tofu without oil, breaking it up into small pieces with a wooden spatula. Continue until all the moisture is evaporated, about 5 minutes.

❷ *Add Protein and Vegetables* » Add about ½ tablespoon of oil and tuna if using, then add chopped **Nimono Base** to the skillet. Mix well to coat the tofu and vegetables with oil.

❸ *Season and Add Eggs* » Drizzle soy sauce and *sake* over the mixture and mix well. Add chopped green onions. Pour the beaten eggs onto the tofu mixture in a circular motion, then stir continuously with a whisk until the tofu and egg mixture gets fluffy, about 1 to 2 minutes. Taste and adjust seasoning. Serve hot.

Takikomi-Gohan (Japanese Mixed Rice with Root Vegetables)

Traditionally in Japan, there are two ways to prepare mixed rice dishes. *Takikomi-Gohan* means "cooked together with rice": Raw ingredients, seasonings, and rice are cooked together. *Maze-Gohan* means "mixed rice": Seasoned, ready-to-eat vegetables, chicken, and/or seafood are mixed into cooked rice. This recipe is a combination of both, which I think tastes best.

While the cook-together method results in well-seasoned rice and ingredients, the mix-later version is much more flexible and allows more variety, especially for single people. Simply heat both cooked rice and chopped *Nimono* Base, then mix with tuna, soy sauce, *sake*, and a bit of *dashi* (if you have any).

Either way, if you make extra, freeze by dividing it into individually-sized rice balls. Reheat them completely before eating. They are great for lunches and snacks.

Serves 4

- ▶ 2 cups *sushi* rice
- ▶ 2¼ cups water or *dashi (p.74)* stock (or water with a 3-inch square dried *kombu*)
- ▶ 1 to 2 tablespoons soy sauce
- ▶ 1 tablespoon *sake*
- ▶ Optional: ½ to 1 tablespoon *mirin*
- ▶ 1 cup to 1½ cups NIMONO BASE *(p.46)*, chopped in smaller pieces (about ½ inch cubes or smaller)
- ▶ Optional: ½ can tuna, preferably in olive oil (about ¼ cup), crumbled with a fork

❶ *Prepare and Season Rice* » Rinse rice in cold water a few times until the water runs clear. Add soy sauce, *sake, mirin,* and *dashi* (or *kombu* and water) to rice, up to the 2-cup line of the rice cooker, and soak for about 20 to 30 minutes *(See note below about rice cooker cup measurements)*.

❷ *Cook Rice* » Start the rice cooker. If you don't have a rice cooker, bring the rice and water to a boil in a medium pan. Cover, and simmer for 15 minutes or until the water is all absorbed. Turn off heat.

❸ *Add "Ready-To-Go" Ingredients* » Quickly mix the Nimono Base and tuna (if using) into the cooked rice and cover immediately to keep the steam in as much as possible. Let it steam for another 10 minutes. This will warm up even cold vegetables. Adjust seasoning if needed. Serve hot.

Note: When you are using a rice cooker, be sure to measure the rice using the cup that came with it, and add the water to the line that indicates the amount. A typical rice cooker cup is 180 cc, but a regular American cup is 240 cc. If you mix them up, you get either soggy or crunchy rice. If you don't have the cup that came with the rice cooker, use a regular measuring cup and be sure to use 1⅛ cup water for every cup of rice.

Tip: Soaking rice is the proper Japanese way to cook perfect rice. If you want to skip this, use lukewarm liquid and add a pinch of sugar to cook rice.

FLEXIPE BASE 5.

Mirepoix Base:

Sautéed Onion, Carrot, and Celery

- *Mirepoix Pilaf*
  (Fried Rice with Vegetables)
- Stuffed Summer Vegetables
- Stuffed Cabbage Rolls
- KWIK Chili
- KWIK Bolognese Sauce
  with Linguine

Mirepoix Base: Sautéed Onion, Carrot, and Celery

Mirepoix is a flavor base made with aromatic vegetables used regularly, especially at French restaurants, for stocks and sauces. It seems daunting to chop all the vegetables, but if you cut them into 1-inch pieces, and pulse each vegetable in a food processor to ¼ inch size, it's a snap. Make a large batch and you'll set yourself up for an endless number of tasty dishes in a fraction of the time—especially if you keep it ready to go in the freezer.

The *Mirepoix* base is divided into 3 base "stages". The first stage is onion + carrot + celery; the second stage adds meat; and the third stage adds tomatoes. After each stage, take some out and store separately so that you can use it for different purposes later on. You can either do all the stages at once, or later in the week.

STAGE 1: Mirepoix Base
Makes about 3 cups

- ▶ 2 tablespoons extra virgin olive oil
- ▶ 2 medium onions (about 1 pound), chopped small, about ¼ inch
- ▶ 3 carrots (about ½ pound), chopped small, about ¼ inch (roughly half the amount of onion)
- ▶ 2 stalks celery (about ½ pound), chopped small, about ¼ inch (roughly the same amount as carrots)
- ▶ Salt and pepper

❶ *Sauté Onion, Carrot and Celery* » Heat oil in a large skillet on medium-high heat. Sauté the chopped onions with a little salt until translucent, then add carrots and cook for a minute or two. Add celery and cook until the vegetables sweat and are crisp-tender. Taste. Since you will be adding uncooked sausages (which are often salty) at next stage, I recommend you keep this only lightly seasoned.

Uses: Sautéed Mirepoix is a great addition to salad dressings, sandwich spreads, stuffing, steaks, chicken, fish, risotto, soups, and sauces. It can be used to dress up seared ahi tuna or *crudo* (Italian-style *sashimi*) by mixing with some extra virgin olive oil and balsamic vinegar, OR extra virgin olive oil and soy sauce. You can be adventurous and mix with cream cheese for a healthier, tastier spread for bagels, crackers, and bread!

STAGE 2: Mirepoix Meat Base
Makes about 5 cups

- ▶ 1½ pounds, high-quality uncooked Italian sausage (casings removed) or ground meat
- ▶ 2 cups (⅔ recipe) **MIREPOIX BASE (STAGE 1)**
- ▶ 1 tablespoon extra virgin olive oil

❶ *Add Meat and Brown* ›› Add uncooked sausage to **Mirepoix Base (Stage 1)**, and cook until meat is brown. Taste and adjust seasoning. Since sausages are generously seasoned, you shouldn't have to add any salt.

Note: If using ground meat, add salt, pepper and your favorite spices or herbs at the beginning, mix well and let it stand for a while to boost the flavor. Alternately, use about a ½-inch squeeze of anchovy paste or a dash of fish sauce as you cook the meat. Taste and adjust seasoning.

Uses: Pastas, soups, stir-fried vegetables. Stuffing for vegetables, ravioli, squid.

STAGE 3: Mirepoix Tomato Base
Makes about 6 cups, enough for making both Bolognese and Chili for 4

- ▶ 3½ cups (⅔ recipe) **MIREPOIX MEAT BASE (STAGE 2)**
- ▶ 1 can (28 ounces) chopped tomatoes
- ▶ Salt and pepper
- ▶ Optional: 2 teaspoons tomato paste
- ▶ Optional: 1-inch squeeze of anchovy paste

❶ *Add Tomatoes and Reduce* ›› Add a can of tomatoes to **Mirepoix Meat Base (Stage 2)**. Cook down until thickened and flavor is developed for about 20 to 30 minutes. Taste and adjust seasoning with salt and pepper.

Optional: Add about ½ tablespoon of tomato paste and about 1-inch squeeze of anchovy paste as additional flavor enhancers.

Uses: Bolognese sauce for pasta, ravioli, gnocchi, lasagna, cannelloni. Dishes that use tomato-based meat sauces such as chili, sloppy joe, shepherd's pie, etc. To use this as a base for drier sauces or stuffing, simply use a slotted spoon to drain out the liquid first.

Mirepoix

Mirepoix Pilaf (Fried Rice with Vegetables)

Pilafs are rice dishes typically made by sautéing raw vegetables and rice in oil or butter, then adding liquid and cooking until all the moisture is absorbed into the rice. This usually takes at least 30 minutes. This *Mirepoix Pilaf* is comparable and takes only about 5 minutes. You can also microwave it all together with a little bit of white wine until the rice is hot. Then fluff it up with a fork. This recipe uses brown rice for added nutrition. Also delicious with white rice or quinoa.

Tip: You can use frozen *Mirepoix* in this dish. Directly add it to heated olive oil on high heat, break it up, and add rice.

Serves 2 to 3

▶ **2 cups cooked brown rice (if cold, heat first for best results)**

▶ **About 1 cup MIREPOIX or MIREPOIX MEAT BASE (p.52, 53)**

▶ **1 tablespoon extra virgin olive oil**

▶ **Optional: ½ tablespoon butter**

▶ **Salt and pepper**

▶ **Parsley, chopped**

❶ *Cook Rice and Vegetables* » Heat extra virgin olive oil in a non-stick pan or wok until hot over high heat. Add **Mirepoix Base** and rice. Stir thoroughly until well combined and cooked through. Taste, add butter, and adjust seasoning. Serve hot with chopped parsley on top (optional).

Note: To make this a more substantial, stand-alone dish, sauté about ½ cup cooked chicken, shrimp, or vegetables before adding **Mirepoix Base**, and increase the amount of rice to 2½ to 3 cups.

Stuffed Summer Vegetables

In warmer months, I make different types of stuffed vegetables such as stuffed zucchini flowers and peppers. You can certainly use some of the *Mirepoix Pilaf* leftover *(page 54)* as the stuffing. It's really fun and easy to experiment with multiple fillings and see what you like best. Don't worry about the exact amount; just mix and match and have fun creating different versions. Be sure to taste the filling first and adjust ingredients and seasonings. Trust your taste buds—they will tell you what you need to add, if anything.

Allow about 3 medium-sized vegetables for 2 people, either one kind or a mix. If you end up with extra filling, roll it into small balls and fry or bake them as a snack. It's a cook's treat! The same mixture works for stuffed pasta or squid.

Tip: Pre-heat the oven, if using the regular oven. You do not have to pre-heat the toaster oven.

Serves 2 to 3

▶ 3 to 4 medium size seasonal vegetables: tomato, zucchini, squash blossom, pepper, Italian or Japanese eggplant, etc.

▶ ½ cup **MIREPOIX or MIREPOIX MEAT BASE** *(p.52, 53)*

▶ ½ to 1 cup one of the following: breadcrumbs, cooked rice, couscous, ricotta cheese, etc.

▶ Total ¼ cup one or more of the following: cooked meat, cheese, chopped nuts

▶ Optional: Pesto, minced herbs, or lemon zest to taste

▶ 1 beaten egg

▶ Extra virgin olive oil

▶ Salt and pepper

▶ Optional: Grated cheese

❶ *Prepare Vegetables* » If using squash blossoms, remove the stems and stamens while keeping it whole, rinse gently with water, and pat dry. For other vegetables, cut in half, lengthwise. Scoop out the seeds of tomato, zucchini, and peppers. Sprinkle salt and pepper and drizzle a little olive oil on all sides.

❷ *Prepare Filling* » Combine the Mirepoix Base with different combination of grains, meat, cheese, pesto, etc. and use beaten egg as a binder. Chop tomato and zucchini pulp and seeds (if small) and add to the mixture. Taste and adjust seasoning with salt and pepper.

❸ *Stuff Vegetables and Cook* » Stuff the vegetables with Mirepoix Base mixture. Optional: Sprinkle top with grated cheese. Place them in an oven-proof dish and bake at 400 F about 20 to 30 minutes. Or pan-fry both sides in a non-stick skillet—stuffed side first—until they are cooked through and the top is golden brown, about 5 to 7 minutes each side. Serve hot.

Note: If using squash blossoms, do not bake, always pan-fry. They will cook a lot faster than other vegetables.

Mirepoix

Stuffed Cabbage Rolls

When the weather gets cold, I crave warm stuffed cabbage rolls—my childhood favorite and one of the most popular dishes in Japanese homes. The problem is, making them from scratch requires cumbersome preparation and long simmering. I figured out a quicker and tastier way with my *Mirepoix* Base and my trick: Microwaving a whole cabbage.

Since my Stuffed Cabbage Rolls use rice and *Mirepoix* in the stuffing, each roll contains half the amount of meat of typical recipes, making the stuffing fluffier and healthier. Omit the meat and use vegetable stock to make it vegetarian.

You can even make it easier if you have *Mirepoix Pilaf* leftovers on hand *(page 54)*.

Tip: To make this even healthier, use whole grains such as quinoa instead of rice, and even more vegetables. If there's any cabbage left over, chop it up and use in soups, salads, and stuffing for *gyoza (page 72)*.

Serves 4

- ▶ About 2 cups leftover **Mirepoix Pilaf** *(p.54)* **OR** 1 cup **MIREPOIX or MIREPOIX MEAT BASE** *(p.52, 53)* and 1 cup cooked rice
- ▶ Optional: ¼ cup Parmesan or Pecorino Romano cheese
- ▶ 1 egg, beaten
- ▶ Salt and pepper
- ▶ 1 head cabbage, about 1 to 1½ pounds, outer leaves removed
- ▶ 1 cup canned, chopped tomatoes or 2 large ripe tomatoes, chopped and drained
- ▶ About 2 cups chicken or vegetable broth
- ▶ Optional: Heavy cream or plain yogurt (Greek style or drained)

❶ *Cook Cabbage* » Carefully cut a deep cone-shaped section around the core with a paring knife, and twist it out. Stuff the hole with a damp paper towel. Cover completely with plastic wrap, or place in a covered microwavable container, and microwave on high about 3 minutes. Flip over, and cook another 3 minutes. This will allow you to peel off the leaves and wrap filling more easily. (*Tip:* This is based on a 1 pound cabbage. Adjust the time depending on the size of yours, and the power of your microwave. If it doesn't seem well-steamed, cook a few more minutes.)

❷ *Prepare Filling* » Combine leftover *Mirepoix Pilaf* with beaten egg and mix well. Or mix equal parts of cooked rice and **Mirepoix or Mirepoix Meat Base**, egg, and cheese. Taste and season well.

❸ *Assemble Cabbage Rolls* » **(a)** Remove the hard rib from the base of each cabbage leaf with a knife to make it easier to roll. Sprinkle salt on each cabbage leaf first, place about ¼ cup of the rice mixture onto the middle of each leaf. **(b)** Fold in the front, **(c)** then fold both sides, and roll up tightly. **(d)** Secure the loose end of the cabbage with a toothpick.

(*Tip:* If you don't have toothpicks, 2 pieces of broken spaghetti stuck through the seam works wonders.) **(e)** With all seams on the bottom, arrange the cabbage rolls into a deep, 2 to 3 quart pan as tightly as possible in one or two layers, trying not to leave any space so that they will not unravel during cooking. If there's any space, stuff with leftover cabbage leaves. Break off the top of the spaghetti if it sticks out too much to allow the lid to sit right on top of the cabbage rolls in the next step.

❹ *Add Broth and Cook* » **(f)** Top with chopped tomatoes, and add broth to barely cover the cabbage rolls. If you don't have enough broth, add a little bit of water. Place a lid or plate that is one size smaller than the opening to keep them submerged. Bring to a boil, then maintain a lively simmer for a minimum of 20 minutes. (If you are short on time, arrange cabbage rolls in a microwavable container; cover, microwave them in several minute increments, or use pressure cooker.) Take out rolls carefully with a serving spoon, trying not to tear the cabbage. Serve immediately with tomatoes and cream or yogurt on top.

KWIK Chili

With *Mirepoix* Tomato Base, you can quickly make flavorful chili with any beans and vegetables you have on hand. Don't worry too much about the exact amounts. Trust your taste buds and how your chili looks. For the best results, when using several kinds of vegetables, make sure that they are cut in roughly the same size for even cooking.

Tip: For a dish like this that requires slow simmering, I recommend making a habit of setting a timer on the stove, so that you can focus on another dish while your chili is cooking. Make sure to 1) set the time a little shorter than you think, 2) partially cover the lid, and/or 3) use slightly lower heat so that your food will not burn.

Serves 4

- ▶ About 3 cups **MIREPOIX TOMATO BASE** *(p.53)*
- ▶ 1 can (about 2 cups) cooked beans such as kidney, cannellini, chickpeas, etc.
- ▶ 2 cups assorted vegetables you have on hand, diced into about ½ inch
- ▶ About 1 to 2 cups chicken broth, bean cooking liquid, or water to barely cover the beans and vegetables
- ▶ 1 teaspoon (or more) dried chili powder
- ▶ 1 teaspoon cumin
- ▶ 1 teaspoon dried oregano
- ▶ Optional: ½ cup corn
- ▶ Salt and pepper
- ▶ Optional: Hot sauce
- ▶ Chili topping of your choice (chopped onions, sour cream, shredded cheese, etc.)

❶ *Combine Vegetables, Beans, and Broth* » Combine cooked beans, diced vegetables (about ½ inch or smaller, otherwise, it will take longer to cook) and **Mirepoix Tomato Base** in a medium pan. Add broth or water until the mixture is barely covered.

❷ *Add Mexican Seasonings and Simmer* » Bring to a boil, taste and season with chili powder, cumin, oregano, salt and pepper. Reduce heat and maintain lively simmer for about 15 minutes or more, until flavor is fully developed.

❸ *Serve Hot* » Add corn a few minutes before turning off the heat (optional). Taste and adjust seasoning with salt, pepper, and hot sauce. Serve immediately with sides of chopped onions, sour cream, shredded cheese, and any other chili toppings that appeal to you.

KWIK Bolognese Sauce with Linguine

There is only 1 step to make this traditional Italian sauce. It's perfect for pasta, lasagna, and even shepherd's pie. I even use the leftover for my version of an Afghan dish called *Aushak*—chive raviolis topped with this sauce and yogurt. It's delicious!

Simmering time depends on how much *Mirepoix* Tomato Base *(page 53)* was reduced when you made it, and your personal preference. If you are short on time, a total of 15 to 20 minutes will do. Use only the tomatoes and not the juice (use a slotted spoon), and boost flavor with a ½ cube of chicken or beef bouillon, or ½ teaspoon fish sauce. Reduce the sauce at medium-high heat, stirring frequently.

Serves 4

- ► 1 tablespoon extra virgin olive oil
- ► 2 cloves garlic, crushed
- ► ½ to 1 teaspoon chili peppers
- ► About 3 cups MIREPOIX TOMATO BASE *(p.53)*
- ► 2 tablespoons chopped fresh basil and/or oregano (or 1 teaspoon dried)
- ► About ¼ cup red wine
- ► About ½ cup milk or ¼ cup cream
- ► Salt and pepper
- ► ⅔ to ¾ bag (11 to 12 ounces) linguine or spaghetti
- ► Optional: Grated Parmigiano-Reggiano or Pecorino Romano cheese

❶ *Add Italian Seasonings to Mirepoix Tomato Base and Reduce* » Heat extra virgin olive oil in a sauce pan over medium heat, cook crushed garlic and chili peppers until fragrant and lightly browned. Add **Mirepoix Tomato Base** and bring to a boil, then add herbs, red wine and milk or cream and simmer uncovered and reduce the sauce for about 30 minutes or more. Taste and adjust seasoning. Use this in any Italian dish that calls for tomato-based meat sauce.

Tip: For additional flavor boost, add about ½ tablespoon tomato paste, ½ teaspoon anchovy paste or fish sauce, and/or the rind of Parmigiano-Reggiano or Pecorino Romano cheese when simmering.

❷ *Boil Pasta in Salty Water* » Cook the noodles in plenty of well-salted, boiling water (should taste like seawater, 1 tablespoon salt to 2 to 3 quarts of water). Do not add oil, unless you are cooking wide pasta such as lasagna. Stir well immediately so that they won't stick. Cook 1 minute shorter than package instruction. Fish out the pasta with tongs, or reserve about 1 cup of cooking liquid and drain in a colander. Do not rinse pasta.

❸ *Cook Pasta with Sauce* » Add the pasta and about ½ cup or more of reserved cooking liquid to the sauce to help the sauce adhere to the noodles. Mix well and continue to cook about 1 minute. Serve immediately with grated cheese.

Mirepoix

Marinated Chicken Base:

Garlic, Ginger, or Lemon

- Chicken Roulade (Rolled-Up Chicken with Wine Sauce)

- *Shoga-Yaki* (Chicken Ginger)

- *Kuwayaki Donburi* (Rice Bowl with Sweet Soy Chicken)

Everyone loves chicken. Using a simple marinade will make your chicken succulent and flavorful, and extend its shelf life. It will keep well for a few days in the refrigerator or about a month in the freezer. For time savings and best results, I recommend cutting the thickness by half or slicing about 1 inch wide, especially when you are using breast meat, so that the chicken will cook faster and more evenly.

When freezing, use a few re-sealable freezer bags, separate each sliced piece of marinated chicken as much as possible, and freeze flat. In this way, you can take only the amount you need and cook without thawing.

This marinated chicken can be used for any chicken recipe, from poaching to grilling to deep-frying.

Garlic: Best for European and Mediterranean dishes; grilling

Ginger: Best for Asian dishes; poached chicken (*page 23*)

Lemon: Best for Mediterranean and Middle Eastern dishes; salads

Makes about 1½ pounds, enough for all 3 of the following recipes for 2 people

- ► **1½ pounds boneless skinless chicken breast or thigh**
- ► **1½ teaspoons salt**
- ► **Aromatics: 3 cloves garlic, sliced; OR 1 inch ginger, sliced; OR 1 small lemon, juiced or sliced**
- ► **1½ tablespoons extra virgin olive oil**

❶ *Marinate Chicken* ≫ Mix salt, oil, and aromatics in a quart-size re-sealable freezer bag, and add chicken. Seal the bag. Massage the chicken in the bag so that the oil and flavor will be well distributed. Let the chicken marinate for about 15 minutes. You can use it right away for the following recipes, or use with your favorite chicken preparation. Or take the air out of the bag and store it in the refrigerator for up to 3 days, or the freezer up to 1 month.

How to pan-fry chicken without thawing:

❶ *Cook Frozen Chicken, Covered* ≫ Heat about 1 teaspoon of oil, sprinkle about 1 tablespoon of white wine or *sake* on the chicken, and cook at medium heat with the lid on the pan for about 3 to 5 minutes, depending on the thickness.

❷ *Cook the Other Side, Uncovered* ≫ Uncover, flip the chicken, and cook the other side until both sides are golden brown and the meat is cooked through, about 5 to 7 minutes, depending on the thickness. To check, make a small incision in the thickest part of the meat. If the inside is still raw, cook a few minutes longer. If only a slight trace of pink is visible, cover again, turn off the heat, and leave the chicken in the pan for a few minutes to let it cook with carry-over heat.

Chicken Roulade (Rolled-Up Chicken with Wine Sauce)

You can roll pretty much any cooked vegetables you want, including the *Mirepoix* Base *(page 52)* or chopped Mushroom Base *(page 34)*. Or some cheese, or even a piece of prosciutto. You can also add Tomato and Onion Base *(page 28)* with or without wine and make Chicken Roulade with Tomato Sauce *(as shown in the photo above)*.

Butterflied and pounded breast meat is easier to roll and more elegant, yet thigh meat is more flavorful. Try both. Either way, it looks fancy, it's delicious, and it's super easy!

Note: If the meat is frozen, thaw it first before making this dish.

Serves 2

▶ **½ pound** MARINATED CHICKEN BASE: GARLIC or LEMON *(p.62)*

▶ **½ cup *Mirepoix* Base** *(p.52)* and/or mushrooms, leeks, or other cooked vegetables (cut small or thin)

▶ **About 1 tablespoon flour for dusting**

▶ **⅓ to ½ cup white wine (or ¼ cup each of red wine and stock)**

▶ **½ tablespoon extra virgin olive oil**

▶ **Salt and pepper**

▶ **Optional: Parsley, chopped**

❶ *Prepare Chicken* » If using breast meat, cut the thickness in half so that it'll be easier to roll and will cook faster. If you have time, place meat (either breast or thigh) between two sheets of plastic wrap; pound the meat with a meat pounder, small pan, or rolling pin to ¼ inch thickness for an elegant look and easier rolling.

❷ *Assemble Chicken* » Spread 2 to 3 tablespoons of the sautéed vegetables on each piece of chicken and roll up tightly. If using thigh meat that's not pounded, tie each roll with one or two kitchen twines securely. Dust flour on all sides. Pat off excess flour, if any.

Tip: Use a mesh tea infuser or small, fine sieve to apply flour evenly, and to minimize the amount of mess.

❸ *Brown Chicken, All Sides* » Heat oil in a non-stick or cast-iron skillet until hot. Place the chicken seam-side down, and press it down to seal the seam by searing. Cook and rotate while pressing and searing each part of the seam until all sides are golden brown. Drain the fat from the skillet, if needed.

❹ *De-glaze to Make Pan Sauce* » Taste and season the chicken with pepper, but no salt—it's already been marinated. Add wine (and stock if using), bring to a boil, cover, and turn down the heat to medium-low. Turn chicken rolls occasionally until they are cooked through and the sauce has thickened, about 7 to 10 minutes. (Pierce each with a skewer in the thickest part—if it goes in easily, it's done.) Slice into ½ inch discs so that the filling is visible, or keep as is. Top with the pan sauce and parsley, and serve hot.

Shoga-Yaki (Chicken Ginger)

Shoga-Yaki (Chicken, Pork, or Fish Ginger) is another favorite in Japanese homes and casual restaurants. This is a great dish to make extra (thus the recipe is for four people, or two people twice) so that you have enough leftovers to make delicious *Kuwayaki Donburi* the next day *(page 65)*. This recipe uses a variation of marinated chicken with ginger. If you already have this base prepared, reduce the amount of soy sauce to 1 tablespoon and grated ginger to 1 teaspoon.

This is delicious with pork loin or firm fish steak such as tuna, swordfish, shark, or yellowtail as well.

Serves 4 (OR 2 for *Shoga-Yaki*, 2 for *Kuwayaki* later)

- ▶ ¾ to 1 pound boneless chicken, OR MARINATED CHICKEN BASE: GINGER *(p.62),* sliced in half to reduce thickness, or cut in 1 inch strips
- ▶ 1½ to 2 tablespoons soy sauce
- ▶ 1 to 1½ tablespoons *sake*
- ▶ 2 teaspoons ginger, grated
- ▶ 1 tablespoon corn or potato starch
- ▶ ½ tablespoon vegetable or sesame oil

❶ *Prepare Meat* » Marinate the chicken in soy sauce, *sake,* and ginger for 5 minutes or longer in a bowl or re-sealable plastic bag. Pat dry and dust the cornstarch on both sides of the meat.

Tip: Use a mesh tea infuser, or small fine sieve, or shake the meat with starch in a clean plastic bag to achieve even application with minimum mess.

❷ *Pan-fry Meat* » Heat oil in a non-stick or cast iron skillet until hot. Cook the meat on both sides until golden brown over medium-high heat. Taste and adjust seasoning if needed. Serve hot with steamed rice and a side of cooked vegetables.

Kuwayaki Donburi (Rice Bowl with Sweet Soy Chicken)

This is a great dish to make with leftover *Shoga-Yaki* (chicken, pork, or fish—*page 64*). You can also use the leftover *Nimono* Base *(page 46)*. See how the variety multiplies? In Japan, these rice dishes are served in specially made, larger rice bowls. A deep cereal, soup or café au lait bowl will work as well.

Tip: To toast a sheet of *nori*, use tongs and wave directly above the high heat of a gas or electric stove quickly—1 to 2 seconds—a few times until the color starts to change to dark green. Or, place *nori* on a plate and microwave on high for 10 to 15 seconds per sheet. Once done, take the plate of *nori* out immediately to let it crisp up.

Serves 2

▶ ⅓ to ½ pound *SHOGA-YAKI (p.64)*

▶ 1 tablespoon soy sauce

▶ 1 tablespoon sugar

▶ 1 tablespoon *mirin*

▶ 1 to 1½ tablespoons water

▶ ½ cup or more **Nimono** Base *(p.46)* or pre-prepped green vegetables, such as green beans, okra, or snow peas

▶ 2 cups hot steamed *sushi* rice

▶ Optional: ½ sheet *nori* (the *sushi* wrapping seaweed; available in the Asian food section of well-stocked markets)

▶ Optional: 1 to 2 *ao-shiso* leaves (green perilla)

❶ *Prepare Chicken* » Slice the leftover *Shoga-Yaki* into bite-size pieces.

❷ *Cook Meat with Pan Sauce* » Heat the oil in a medium-sized skillet over medium-high heat. Cook the chicken and vegetables for a few minutes. Add the soy sauce, sugar, *mirin*, and water. Reduce the sauce for a few minutes and coat the meat and vegetables well.

❸ *Serve Hot on Rice* » Place hot steamed rice in a bowl about ⅔ full. Top with toasted nori torn into small pieces, and julienned *ao-shiso* leaves if using, then with the sweet soy chicken, and place the vegetables on the side. Serve immediately.

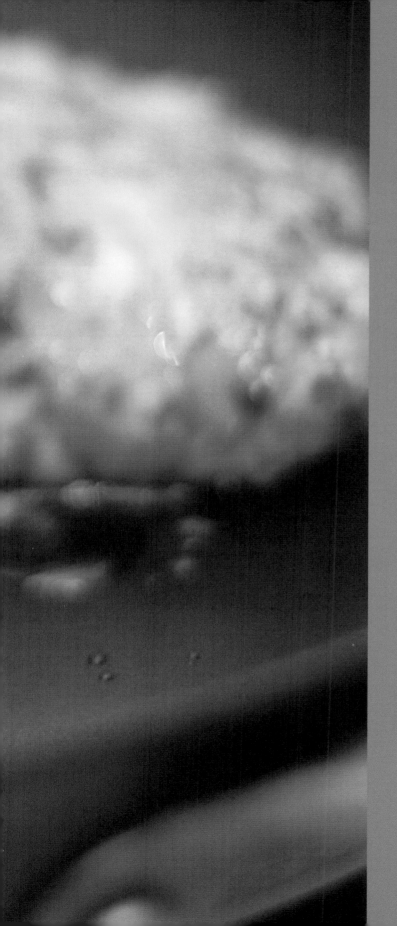

FLEXIPE BASE 7.

Asian Meat Base

- Lettuce Wrap
- Chinese Meatball Soup
- *Gyoza* (Pot-Stickers)

FLEXIPE BASE 7. Asian Meat Base

This is an example of a Flexipe base that I make in a large batch. Most are immediately frozen in single-use portions. Whenever I'm in the mood for an Asian dish that calls for ground meat, I'll grab one portion, thaw and add fresh ingredients, and *Voila!* Dinner is ready! It's handy for any Asian dishes that call for ground meat, not just for stuffing for dumplings such as *wonton* and *shiumai*, but also for meatballs, stir-fries, and toppings for *tofu*, vegetables, and noodles.

By using exactly the same method, you can make different meat bases with any ground meat, different aromatics, and seasonings. For maximum versatility, season it as simply as possible (salt, pepper, oil, a little aromatics, and/or wine so that the meat stays moist and flavorful even after freezing), and add the special seasonings and spices only in the amount you use for a particular cuisine.

Having these in the freezer ready to go is a huge psychological relief when you come home tired and hungry.

Tip: Once frozen, the seasoning often cures the meat. Make sure to season lightly.

Makes about 2 cups

- ► **1 pound ground pork, turkey, or chicken**
- ► **½ bunch green onion, chopped small about ¼ inch (about ½ cup)**
- ► **½ inch fresh ginger, peeled and minced (about 1 tablespoon)**
- ► **1 to 2 tablespoons *sake* or sherry**
- ► **Optional: ½ tablespoon sesame oil (add this for best flavor and juiciness, especially when using poultry)**
- ► **Optional: 1 teaspoon fish sauce (add this for best flavor, especially when using poultry)**
- ► **Salt and pepper**

❶ *Mix Ingredients* » Mix all ingredients thoroughly in a large bowl, directly on a cutting board, or in a plastic bag as in the photo above.

❷ *Package Individually* » Put aside the portion you don't plan to use immediately, divide it into ½ to 1 cup amounts, wrap each tightly with plastic wrap. If not using right away, freeze in a re-sealable freezer bag for up to 1 month. Or make Frozen Flexipe Flats *(p.18)*.

A Note about Salt

Salt gets a bad rap, primarily because of the excessive added sodium in processed foods, but many professional chefs believe that learning to salt food properly is the most important skill in the kitchen.

The ideal saltiness for most dishes is considered to be 0.8 to 0.9% (the sodium ratio to all the other ingredients used in a dish), which is about the same as the saltiness of human blood. (Interesting, isn't it?) When you add salt to something, remember this as a guideline. However, you must also take into account any salt that already exists in food—both naturally and due to processing.

I recommend using kosher or sea salt for cooking. Iodized salt is more common, yet it leaves a chemical flavor. Always taste your food frequently while you are preparing it.

I can't stress this enough! As you may have noticed in most of my recipes, I like adding a little salt (not all 0.8%) at the beginning of the cooking process.

As salt gets absorbed into food, the natural flavor of the ingredients becomes intensified, and it releases moisture and helps the ingredients (especially vegetables) cook faster. Salt also reduces the amount of oil needed for cooking.

By learning to salt food earlier in the cooking process, and season as I go, the flavor of my food drastically improved. So will yours.

Lettuce Wrap

A favorite at Chinese restaurants, a lettuce wrap is like a mini burrito wrapped in lettuce instead of a tortilla.

For this dish, choose larger, softer, or rounder leafed lettuce such as Boston, butter, green leaf, red leaf, or iceberg. I like the crunchiness of romaine, but it's not as easy to keep the filling inside. Be sure to have some napkins handy!

Depending on the size, you may only need half of the lettuce. Keep the rest in a sealed container, and use for salads within a few days.

Tip: Wrapping all the leaves in a few sheets of moist paper towel first will keep them fresh and green longer.

I encourage you to play with different flavors, but if you are not sure, use exactly the same seasoning as my *gyoza* filling: 1 tablespoon *sake* and sesame oil, ½ to 1 tablespoon each of soy sauce and fish sauce, and 1 teaspoon sugar.

This meat and vegetable mixture is also delicious on steamed rice, cooked noodles, or *tofu*. Or use as a stuffing for spring rolls.

Serves 2 to 3

- ► 1 head lettuce, separated, washed and dried well
- ► Total 1 to 2 cups assorted vegetables you have on hand, diced into about ¼ to ½ inch
- ► 1 cup ASIAN MEAT BASE *(p.68)*
- ► Optional: 1 clove garlic, minced
- ► Condiments of your choice: soy sauce, fish sauce, oyster sauce, chili sauce, *kimchi* juice, ketchup, *miso*, honey, etc.
- ► Salt and pepper
- ► Optional: About 1 cup steamed rice, mint, and/or cilantro

❶ *Prepare Vegetables* » Wash separated lettuce leaves, and dry them in a salad spinner or a kitchen towel. Set aside. Chop your favorite vegetables, about ½ cup or more per person (1:1 or 2:1 ratio with the meat).

❷ *Cook Meat and Vegetables* » Heat 1 teaspoon of sesame oil in a medium-size skillet over medium-high heat, sauté garlic if using, add Asian Meat Base, and cook until the meat is no longer pink. Add vegetables in the order of hardness and time needed to cook.

❸ *Season* » Mix in your favorite Asian condiments. Start with about 1 teaspoon each of a few of the condiments (remember the 0.8% guideline), taste, and adjust seasoning.

❹ *Wrap Meat with Lettuce and Eat* » Serve hot or room temperature with lettuce, extra condiments, herbs, and/or steamed rice on the side.

Chinese Meatball Soup

This recipe is so easy that it's practically Kitchen Wizard magic! Once you've made the Asian Meat Base, make Frozen Flexipe Flats: Spread about 1 cup to about ¼ to ⅓ inch thickness in a quart-size re-sealable freezer bag. Score a 1-inch grid with a chopstick or the straight side of a spatula. Freeze flat.

Then whenever you feel like some Chinese Meatball Soup, you can pull a bag of the frozen Asian Meat Base out of the freezer and break off squares directly into boiling broth. Cook with whatever vegetables you have on hand for nutritious, fast, and satisfying soup any time of the day.

Tip: If using a fresh meat mixture, allow about ¼ cup per person, and drop ½ to 1 tablespoon portion at a time into the boiling soup. You can also use leftover *gyoza* (page 72) in place of meatballs.

Serves 2

▸ Total 1 cup assorted vegetables you have on hand, cut into bite-size pieces

▸ 2 cups chicken broth (OR 2 cups water with 2 slices of ginger, 1 tablespoon *sake*, and 1 teaspoon fish sauce)

▸ ½ cup ASIAN MEAT BASE *(p.68)*, frozen or fresh

▸ Salt and pepper

▸ Fish sauce and/or soy sauce to taste

▸ Optional: Sesame oil and/or chili oil

▸ Optional: 1 egg, beaten

▸ Optional: Green onion, chopped

❶ *Prepare Vegetables* » Cut about ½ cup total per person of your favorite fast-cooking vegetables into bite-size pieces. (Spinach, Napa cabbage, tomatoes, *shiitake* mushrooms, broccoli, asparagus, etc.)

❷ *Add Meatballs and Vegetables into Soup* » Bring chicken broth to a boil in a medium, deep sauce pan over high heat. Break off pieces of frozen Asian Meat Base straight from the bag (about ¼ bag = ¼ cup per person) and add to the boiling soup. Keep the heat on high so that the temperature will not drop. When the soup starts boiling again, add each vegetable, starting with those that take the longest to cook (in other words, the hardest ones first). Adjust the heat to maintain a gentle boil until all vegetables are tender and meat is cooked through. Skim the foam, if there's any developing on the surface, to keep the broth clear.

❸ *Season Soup* » Taste and season with salt and pepper, fish sauce, soy sauce, sesame oil, chili oil, etc. (Remember the 0.8% seasoning guideline!)

❹ *Add Beaten Egg to Soup* » To make egg drop soup, add a pinch of salt to beaten egg, pour the egg in a steady stream in a circular motion into the gently boiling broth. Let it set for a minute, turn off heat, and stir gently with a fork. Serve immediately with ½ tablespoon of chopped green onions on top.

Gyoza (Pot-Stickers)

Gyoza are similar to ravioli—a mixture of minced ingredients such as meat, seafood and/or vegetables wrapped in thin flour-based skins and cooked: pan-fried, deep-fried, steamed, boiled, or in a soup. It is probably one of *the* most popular foods in Japan. It quickly gained popularity after World War II when Japanese expats from Manchuria (including my maternal family) introduced the dish to the mainstream dining scene in their home country. Gyoza are now widely available in the U.S. at restaurants and at supermarkets. Once you experience the fresh home-made version, you will never buy the ready-made kind again! Take advantage of your Asian Meat Base to prepare a typically time-consuming dish like gyoza with much less time and effort. It's easy to enjoy a few different varieties of gyoza by dividing the Asian Meat Base into several bowls and adding different vegetables, seafood, and seasoning.

Gyoza skins or wonton wrappers can be found in the refrigerated or Asian section of well-stocked supermarkets. If there are leftover wrappers, you can make ravioli with them.

Examples of fillings:

Vegetables (with or without meat or seafood): cabbage, Napa cabbage, *shiitake* mushrooms, green onions, Chinese chives, asparagus, spinach, green beans, snow pea spouts, lotus root, celery, green pepper, *tofu*, etc. *Tip:* Use vegetables with lower moisture content, and chop them finely for easier wrapping.

Meat (with vegetables): pork, chicken, turkey, or beef

Seafood (with vegetables; with or without poultry or pork): shrimp, scallops, squid, and/or crab

Note: The moisture in the filling tends to melt the gyoza skin before cooking. Until you have some practice wrapping gyoza, I recommend using vegetables with a low moisture content. If you want to use high-moisture content ingredients like Napa cabbage, sprinkle a generous amount of salt on minced Napa cabbage first, let it sit for about 10 minutes, and squeeze out the extra moisture before mixing with other ingredients. If you use the food processor, make sure to pulse to a coarse chop (about ¼ inch), and drain moisture well before proceeding.

Serves 2 to 3

- ▶ 1 cup **ASIAN MEAT BASE** *(p.68)*
- ▶ Total 1 to 2 cups assorted vegetables and/ or seafood, minced small
- ▶ Optional: 1 clove garlic, minced or grated
- ▶ 1 tablespoon *sake*
- ▶ 1 tablespoon soy sauce
- ▶ ½ tablespoon fish sauce
- ▶ 1 tablespoon sesame oil
- ▶ 1 teaspoon sugar
- ▶ Salt and pepper
- ▶ 1 package gyoza wrappers
- ▶ 2 teaspoons vegetable oil
- ▶ Dipping sauce: soy sauce, rice vinegar, chili oil, etc.

❶ Prepare Filling » Mix thoroughly 1 part Asian Meat Base, 1 or 2 parts minced vegetables and/or seafood, and seasonings (*sake*, soy sauce, fish sauce, sesame oil, sugar, plus garlic if using). Taste and adjust seasoning. (*Tip:* Cook about ½ teaspoon of the mixture in a microwave or skillet, and taste.)

(a)

❷ Wrap Gyoza » Before you start wrapping gyoza, have 1 cup of water, a paper towel, and a flat surface covered with a parchment paper, silicon mat, or thin layer of flour so that gyoza won't stick. Place a gyoza skin on the palm of your non-dominant hand, and top about 1 heaping teaspoon of filling in the center, making sure there's no filling on the edge (it will prevent the skin from sealing). **(a)** Wet the outer edge of the skin with your finger. **(b)** Fold over and pinch the skin tightly **(c)** all around the edge, so that the filling will not come out. Keep them seam-side up while wrapping the rest of the gyoza.

(b)

ADVANCED OPTION *For a more classic, pleated, crescent moon-shaped gyoza:* **(d)** Use your dominant hand and start sealing by pinching and folding in pleats from the outer edge of the gyoza every ½ inch on the front side until you run out of space. **(e)** Make sure that seams are pressed tightly.

(c)

❸ Brown Gyoza » **(f)** Heat oil in a large non-stick skillet, arrange gyoza seam-side up, and cook on high heat until the bottom is golden brown. If you can't fit them all in one, use another skillet.

ADVANCED OPTION

(d)

❹ Steam Gyoza » Add hot water (simply microwave the water you used for wrapping) to about half of the height of the gyoza and cover with a lid. Lower heat to medium and continue to cook for 2 to 3 minutes until the skin is translucent, and filling is visible. Remove the cover, burn off or pour out the water if there's any, and cook another minute to crisp up gyoza.

(e)

❺ Serve Hot with Dipping Sauce » Turn off heat, use a spatula to loosen gyoza, cover with a flat lid (or a plate), and flip the pan over quickly and carefully so that the brown side is on top. Serve hot with your favorite dipping sauce.

Note: You can also boil or steam gyoza instead of frying. When steaming, layer large outer leaves of lettuce or cabbage to cover the bottom of the steamer completely to prevent sticking.

Tip for parents of picky eaters: Gyoza is a great way to sneak in minced vegetables you want your kids to eat. They will love them!

(f)

Asian Meat

Japanese and Asian Ingredients

Investing in a few key Japanese and Asian ingredients is the simple solution to successfully cook ethnic meals at home. These ingredients are not just for Asian food. They are versatile and add deep flavor to your dish. Start with the basics, such as soy sauce, *sake, mirin, miso,* rice vinegar, and/or fish sauce. As you increase your Kitchen Wizarding skills and your Flexipe repertoire, consider adding more of these ingredients to your pantry. You can find most of them at the Asian grocery section of larger supermarkets or Asian markets.

Dashi

Japanese fish stock. There are ready-made liquid and powdered types. Or you can buy *katsuo-bushi* (dried bonito flakes) and/or *kombu* (sea kelp) and make your own. Many people use both bonito flakes and *kombu* for the best flavor. A vegan *dashi* can be made with *kombu* alone.

Kombu (Sea Kelp)

Kombu is dried large sea kelp, high in *umami* and used to make *dashi*, a Japanese broth. For the best flavor, Japanese prefer to use a mixture of *kombu* and bonito flakes for their *dashi*. The fastest way to make *kombu dashi* is to cook a 3-inch square of dried *kombu* in 2 cups of cold water, then take it out when the water starts boiling. Or soak the *kombu* in cold water and leave it alone overnight, and take out the *kombu* before using. Store *dashi* in the refrigerator and use within 2 days, or freeze in an ice tray.

Katsuo-bushi (Bonito Flakes)

Katsuo-bushi is dried bonito flakes, very high in *umami* that adds rich flavor to your dish. Roughly shaved bonito flakes are used to make *dashi*, the Japanese fish broth. Finely shaved bonito flakes are great topping for *tofu*, Japanese noodles, salads, etc. The fastest and easiest way to make *katsuo dashi* is to place a handful of bonito flakes in a heat resistant bowl, and pour 2 cups of boiling water. Leave it alone for 5 minutes, and strain. Store it in the refrigerator and use within 2 days, or freeze in an ice tray.

Fresh Ginger

It adds fragrant spiciness to many Asian dishes. It is considered medicinal. Use fresh ginger root for the best flavor. You can peel the skin and store it in the freezer, then grate it frozen.

Mirin

Sweet cooking wine that adds delicate sweetness and depth of flavor *(umami)*, and also gives luster to sauces and glazes and can help them cling to food. It's also called *hon-mirin (hon* means "authentic" or "real"). *Aji-mirin* has added salt, corn syrup, and water. *Hon-mirin* is highly recommended if it's available. It makes a big difference. Equal amounts of dry sherry and sugar can be used as substitute.

Miso Paste

Fermented soy bean paste that's typically used as a soup base. Red *miso (aka-miso)* is favored in Northern and Eastern Japan (saltier, deeper flavor), while white *miso (shiro-miso)* is used more often in Western Japan (sweeter and more subtle flavor). A combination of these two types is also available called *awase-miso* (meaning "mixed miso"). It's gaining popularity in the U.S. It adds *umami* (depth of flavor) to sauces, stews, and salad dressings.

Rice Vinegar

Delicately flavored vinegar with an acidity of 4%, it tastes milder than other types of vinegar, which are about 6%. A must when making *sushi*, but also great for dressings, pickling, and other dishes. Japanese varieties are preferred (those from Southeast Asia taste significantly different). *Mizkan/Nakano* and *Marukan* are readily available brands.

Sake

Japanese rice wine. For cooking, an inexpensive variety or leftover drinkable *sake* is fine, but I don't recommend "cooking *sake*" because it has added ingredients. Instead, substitute with dry white wine in a pinch.

Soy Sauce

Japanese brands are better for Japanese food, since non-Japanese kinds contain molasses, thus taste sweeter. *Kikkoman* brand is readily available in most supermarkets. *Tamari* (thicker, darker soy sauce made without wheat) is an excellent substitute, especially for those who are gluten-intolerant.

Sesame Oil

It has a deep nutty flavor and is great in many Asian dishes, from seasoning to stir-frying. Dark, roasted sesame oil is preferred for deeper flavor.

Sesame Seeds

Come in white or black, as well as raw, roasted, whole, and ground. The roasted white seeds are a great place to start. When you need ground sesame seeds, use a spice grinder. You can use sesame seeds for non-Asian dishes, such as breads, cookies, and pastries, as well.

Chili Bean Paste

Indispensable seasoning for spicy Sichuan cooking, this paste is made of fava beans and lots of chili. It adds a spicy kick and rich flavor to stir-fries and soups. Depending on the amount of chili used, there are great differences in spiciness. Be sure to taste (lick) first, to determine the amount you want to use in your dish.

Fish Sauce

A must in Thai and Vietnamese cuisine. This light, caramel-colored sauce made of fermented anchovies adds fantastic flavor (*umami*) to Asian and European food alike (especially in Caesar salad dressing!) as a more economical and convenient anchovy substitute. It is extremely pungent so can be overwhelming—use sparingly, especially for non-South Asian dishes.

Garam Masala

Garam means hot, *masala* means mixture. This is a spice blend used in many Indian dishes often with other seasonings such as curry powder. It is very fragrant and spicy, but not hot like chili. Depending on the region, brand, and household, the combination of spices vary. Choose a brand that has a more yellowish color. The redder it is, the hotter, with more cayenne. Easy to make at home by toasting whole spices and grinding them together in the spice mill.

Oyster Sauce

This thick, deep brown sauce used often in stir-fries is made of oyster extract, caramel, corn starch, and salt. It adds a delicious complex flavor, yet doesn't taste or smell fishy. It's very versatile—goes well with beef, chicken, seafood, *tofu*, and noodles. Also use as a dipping sauce for sautéed Asian greens as well as broccoli. Add this toward the end of the cooking for the best flavor. The more expensive, the more oyster extract and less fillers—meaning a much better tasting dish.

Congratulations!

Now that you've learned the secrets to becoming a Kitchen Wizard, start cooking and experimenting! By using Flexipes, your everyday cooking should be much simpler and faster than you ever imagined. You can make hundreds of different freshly prepared dishes with these seven Flexipe bases, mixing and matching with what you have on hand. You will minimize time and waste, while maximizing variety and flavor. How convenient is that? You will surely appear to be a Kitchen Wizard in the eyes of your family and yourself!

Stay connected

I'd love to hear your success stories.

Email: **mari@KitchenWizardMari.com**

Website: **http://KitchenWizardMari.com**

Facebook: **http://Facebook.dj/KitchenWizard**

Twitter: **http://Twitter.com/MariSuzuki**

Want to be healthier in general?

Check out the American Heart Association's Life's Simple Seven: Eat Better, Get Active, Lose Weight, Manage Blood Pressure, Reduce Blood Sugar, Control Cholesterol, and Stop Smoking. To find out where you stand with these goals for healthier life, take the My Life Check assessment at **http://MyLifeCheck.org.**

Want to learn more Flexipes?

- If you live in the Bay Area, I offer in-person demos and hands-on classes.
- I can also develop customized Flexipes for you, using your favorite ingredients.
- Cooking parties make great celebrations for birthdays, showers, team-building events, or get-togethers. Menus can be customized to your group's preferences and cooking abilities.

- **Coaching and Consultations**

  I am also available to consult on menus, menu planning, and shopping lists, as well as hands-on lessons in groups or one-on-one. If you are really serious about getting in gear right away, consider my "Ready-To-Go" Kitchen Makeovers and Culinary Coaching with Flexipe classes.

- **Kitchen Wizard Club**

  The fastest path to becoming a Kitchen Wizard! The members of this unique monthly membership club enjoy regular Kitchen Wizard Q&A calls and tele-seminars so that they will become more efficient and confident in the kitchen. They also receive special discounts on classes and consultations.

For information on any of my programs, please visit **http://KitchenWizardMari.com.**

Be sure to show off the photos of your dinners on my Facebook page at **http://Facebook.dj/KitchenWizard**!

Happy Cooking!

Mari

About Mari Suzuki, the Kitchen Wizard

Mari Suzuki is a cookbook author, cooking optimization expert, trainer, and food blogger. Combining her passions (food, culture, efficiency) and eclectic background (native Japanese, former Systems Engineer at IBM, Global Logistics Consultant at FedEx, and life coach), she designed the Kitchen Wizard Method, a cooking training method based on healthy and efficient modern Japanese culinary wisdom that helps busy people establish sustainable daily cooking habits. She is a member of the American Heart Association's 2020 Task Force Team to help improve the cardiovascular health of all Americans by 20% by 2020 through healthy eating.

Her secrets and the multi-dish, flexible recipes she has developed called Flexipes not only maximize your food and resources while minimizing your time and effort, but also boost your confidence, efficiency, and enjoyment. By following Mari's methods, you too will soon feel like a wizard in the kitchen!